The
KEY
to
ETERNITY

The
KEY
to
ETERNITY

JoAnn Young

CREATION
HOUSE

THE KEY TO ETERNITY by JoAnn Young
Published by Creation House
A Charisma Media Company
600 Rinehart Road
Lake Mary, Florida 32746
www.charismamedia.com

Unless otherwise noted, all Scripture quotations are from the New American Standard Bible—Updated Edition, Copyright © 1960, 1962, 1963, 1968, 1971, 1972, 1973, 1975, 1977, 1995 by The Lockman Foundation. Used by permission. (www.Lockman.org)

Scripture quotations marked NIV are from the Holy Bible, New International Version. Copyright © 1973, 1978, 1984, 2010, 2011, International Bible Society. Used by permission.

Scripture quotations marked NKJV are from the New King James Version of the Bible. Copyright © 1979, 1980, 1982 by Thomas Nelson, Inc., publishers. Used by permission.

Design Director: Bill Johnson
Cover design by Nathan Morgan

Visit the author's website: www.house-of-prayer.org

Library of Congress Cataloging-in-Publication Data: 2011942166
International Standard Book Number: 978-1-61638-742-6
E-book International Standard Book Number: 978-1-61638-743-3

While the author has made every effort to provide accurate telephone numbers and Internet addresses at the time of publication, neither the publisher nor the author assumes any responsibility for errors or for changes that occur after publication.

First edition

11 12 13 14 15 — 987654321
Printed in Canada

ACKNOWLEDGMENTS

This book is dedicated to the Lord Jesus Christ who makes all things possible to them who believe. Christ has given me new eyes of seeing the world and faith to keep looking towards Him. To my fabulous husband, Jerry, whom I love very much; thanks for all that you do and for supporting me and encouraging me with this assignment. I will always love you. To my mother, Leola Bellard, who has encouraged me to live a godly life, I love you. To my mother's husband, Mr. Alvin Bellard, my brothers and sister, Patrick Watson, Donald Watson, Tony Watson, and Pamela Watson, I love you all. To our children, Jessica Green and Leekus Green, God has blessed us with you. To Mary Jane Gonzales, my long-time prayer partner. Thank you for praying this book through. You are a true friend in Christ. Last, but not least, to my loving sister, Kim Lewis, and my father, Emery Watson, who is with the Lord; your temporary departure has helped me to grow closer to God.

DEDICATION

To the Father of Abraham, Isaac,
and Jacob: to the Great I Am:

WHERE CAN I GO

Where can I go
Where Your beauty is not found?
Where shall I go?
Everywhere I go
Displays Your beauty;
Everything I see
Displays Your majesty.
The beauty of Your love is everywhere,
I see it in all things.
Where can I go
Where Your beauty
Is not found?
Nowhere, on the Earth!

LIFTED HIGH

Your Name is lifted High
Above all names.
Your Spirit fills the Earth.
Your glory is everywhere.
My heart loves to give
You praise and adoration;
My lips continually
Sing You praises.
My joy is made complete
In Your love for me.
I love to lift Your Name
On High for all the world to see!

YOUR LOVE

Where does the beauty
Of Your love come from?
Does it come from the ocean,
The wind, the sky?
Your love burns like fire for me;
It is unending, ever consuming,
It radiates through my being.
Your love is everlasting,
It is for eternity,
And it is all for me.
Your love.

CONTENTS

PREFACE

Discover the Key that Leads to Eternity
in Heaven and Fourteen Keys to
Living the Abundant Life Now

The thief comes only to steal and kill and destroy; I came
that they may have life, and have it abundantly.
—JOHN 10:10

The *Key to Eternity* was written as a guide to eternal life,
through Jesus Christ, and as a guide to a blessed and successful life now, until eternity with Christ. It was also written
to equip each of God's people with the knowledge needed to
become an effective and successful person in Christ. It has refer-
ence scriptures to support the different topics discussed. *The Key
to Eternity* is an informative book that demonstrates what the
Bible teaches on the promises of God for every believer in Christ:
our rights as Christians; authority over Satan, sickness, addictions and everything that is contrary to the Word of God.

This book was written for all age groups; those seeking a
closer relationship with Christ and those looking for victory in
their lives.

The Key to Eternity will help you become all you can be in
Christ Jesus, by developing a closer relationship with Him. This

book covers topics such as, how to begin a relationship with Christ, the character of God, who is God, how to hear from God, and how to live a successful life the way God intended. This book explains why God hates doubt in a believer, and it also covers other important issues of life that we as believers have the power to overcome.

This book will strengthen you in your relationship with Christ, as well as equip you with resources to overcome the world's temptations.

Many Christians struggle today because of fear, doubt, or not trusting the words of God. Many people fear the unknown. We want to know every detail, therefore limiting the things that should be surrendered to God. We as humans want to control everything, every aspect of our lives. Surrendering to God can be a threat to some people because it means letting go and allowing God to work by trusting Him with the outcome.

We do not realize and/or believe that God is in total control of everything on earth. Jesus has dominion over everything. He can change our circumstances through prayer. Many do not believe and are not patient enough to see their prayers answered. We do not believe that our prayers will come to pass in God's timing. When we pray, we expect immediate answers or changes concerning our circumstances. However God chooses to change things in our lives or answer the prayer, we must trust Him and wait patiently and expectantly. Sometimes we are impatient and we change the circumstances ourselves; therefore, we miss the miracle God intended.

Chapter 1: God's Plan for Your Life

This chapter explains how to find your divine destiny. You will learn the role of the Holy Spirit and how the Holy Spirit guides you to God's perfect plan. This chapter explains how Jesus' death on the cross allows you to have a relationship with the Father, and how God reveals His plan to you when you surrender to His authority. You will discover how surrendering to God allows the Holy Spirit to lead you into God's perfect will, thus fulfilling our divine purpose in life.

CHAPTER 2: DECEITFUL PRACTICES

This chapter is the grace chapter because it demonstrates God's grace and mercy on us as sinners. It contains examples of what to avoid in our lives that bring physical and spiritual consequences. It explains how God is merciful and gracious in forgiving us by calling us to repent and return to our God-ordained destiny.

The chapter explains how we can open the door for Satan to enter our lives and cause destruction, without us even realizing it. You will discover why putting on the armor of God daily will help you to overcome and be encouraged to stay in God's will.

CHAPTER 3: THE BOOK OF ESTHER REVEALS GOD'S CHARACTER

This chapter explains how obedience brings God's blessings, and disobedience to God can cause us to miss or overlook our blessings in life. It reveals how the king's character in the Book of Esther is an example of God's favor toward believers in Christ who walk in obedience to Him with the guidance of the Holy Spirit. This chapter is an analogy of God's character.

The Bible tells us that obedience is better than a sacrifice (1 Sam. 15:22). Christ dying on the cross is a perfect example of His obedience to God. When the time came for Jesus to go to the cross, He said, "Lord, not my will be done, but yours." (See Luke 22:42.) Because of Christ's obedience we are blessed. In this chapter you will learn how the Jews were blessed because of Esther's obedience to the king and God.

CHAPTER 4: WHO IS GOD?

This chapter describes the character of God and who God is. It explains from a biblical standpoint the ways of God. It reminds us that God is love. He is real. Many people have this idea that God is in heaven looking at every wrong we do. We forget that He is a caring and loving Father who wants the best for His children.

In this chapter you will be encouraged by a personal testimony of how God places angels in our lives for protection and guidance.

The chapter also explains how we can experience His presence and love when we seek Him. God is concerned with every aspect of our life. His Holy Spirit dwells within every born-again believer. The chapter also explains how the Holy Spirit guides us in life and helps us to make right decisions. This chapter will inform you on how to experience the glory and blessings of God.

CHAPTER 5: HOW TO HEAR FROM GOD

This chapter explains the importance of having a relationship with Jesus Christ. Having a personal relationship with Him is the first step in hearing from God. This chapter discusses the different ways God communicates with us. God chooses the way He communicates to us; whether it is through prophets and disciples, directly from God, by the Holy Spirit, through visions and dreams, through angelic visitations, or by signs and wonders.

In this chapter you will discover what faith is and how to strengthen your faith by stirring it, waiting, watching, and expecting your promise. The chapter also explains why many will hear from God during their "burning bush" experience.

Chapter 6: The Key to a Successful Life

This chapter explains the true meaning of success. It is a guide on how to obtain godly success. It deals with the challenges of life and how to make the necessary changes in order to accomplish your divine destiny. The chapter describes the worldly view of success and God's view.

In this chapter you will learn how Jesus paid the price for you to be successful. This chapter also explains the path to salvation; it tells you how to deal with everyday temptations to sin and how the Holy Spirit helps you to overcome those temptations that we all experience.

You will learn how to pray the Scriptures and armor yourself daily against fear, worry, and doubt. You will also learn how to maintain your daily peace that Jesus provides.

Chapter 7: Things You Should Always Remember

In this chapter you are reminded to always be alert of Satan's schemes in your life. You will learn what the Bible tells us about our God-given authority as believers in Christ.

This chapter describes how to follow the Holy Spirit's guidance. It is the Holy Spirit who will enlighten you to the tricks of the enemy. The chapter also reminds us of the consequences of not having God in our lives as our divine protector, healer, and motivator.

The chapter gives you examples of the importance of teaching this generation about the ways of God, how to become a godly generation, and how to be imitators of Christ.

You will discover that you as a believer have power over Satan and his attacks. God has given you authority over all the power of the enemy, Satan.

CHAPTER 8: WORDS OF WISDOM

In this chapter you will be encouraged to depend on and trust Jesus for everything in life and taught how to surrender your life to Him. It emphasizes how we are not alone; Jesus is always at your side waiting for you to call on Him for help or guidance. One way to call upon Him is through prayer. God did not intend for us to be alone in this dark world, but He desires that we seek Him and trust Him to see us through life's challenges.

This chapter also explains how the difficulties of life, if not placed at the feet of Jesus, can lead you to physical and psychological problems. He is our helper. He desires to help us through life's circumstances.

CHAPTER 9: WORDS OF ENCOURAGEMENT

This chapter explains the importance of developing a close relationship with Jesus. He is our encourager. He sent the Holy Spirit to encourage us in times of despair and to reassure us when seeking God's guidance.

The chapter focuses on the importance of spending time with God and meditating in His Word daily. God uses the Scriptures as encouragement to us during difficult times, as well as a guide to know His will for a particular situation.

In this chapter you are reminded of your value to God and how God loves you. He sent His only Son to make atonement for our sins. Through His Son, Jesus, we can have a relationship with God. We can live the abundant life in Christ that God promises in His Word. This chapter also guides you on how to rely on the Holy Spirit to help you overcome strongholds in your life.

CHAPTER 10: THINGS TO DO

This chapter explains the importance of prayer and worship. It describes God's holiness and the importance of forgiveness before entering into His presence. The chapter also explains how God is concerned with every aspect of your life.

CHAPTER 11: WHY THINGS HAPPEN TO US

When unexpected, unfavorable things happen to us, the first thing we ask God is why. This chapter contains answers to questions that everyone has asked at one time or another: Why am I going through this? Why did this happen to me? Why has God allowed this to happen? You will see that God does not cause these things to occur, but He can change the outcome through prayer. Trusting Him during difficult times will give you peace to know that He is taking care of the *"why"* in your life.

The chapter also encourages the reader to seek God and trust Him with circumstances that may come your way, knowing that God will cause everything to work out for your good.

CHAPTER 12: WHY GOD HATES DOUBT

This chapter defines the meaning of doubt and explains why God hates it when we as believers doubt His supernatural abilities and/or His willingness to intercede on our behalf.

The chapter reminds us of our importance to God. It also reiterates our authority over Satan and sickness. The chapter demonstrates how doubting God's power through the work of the Holy Spirit can hinder physical healing and prevent God from changing situations in our lives.

In this chapter you are reminded of the supernatural abilities of our Father, God. You will be encouraged to spend more time in prayer and meditating on the Word of God. It also emphasizes the importance of trusting and believing in God and His promises.

This chapter demonstrates the power of spoken words. You will be encouraged by personal testimonies of physical healings. The chapter also encourages you to stay focused on God and believe that whatever you ask in prayer according to the will of God will come to pass, despite what you see, hear, or feel.

CHAPTER 13: THE UNLIMITED POWER OF GOD

This chapter reminds you of God's unlimited power. It explains why we should not place limits on God, but get out of the box of our everyday thinking by broadening our vision.

We have to think beyond what our eyes can see and expect God to do exceedingly above what we may ask or think as He says in His Word. When we put limits on God we limit our blessings.

The chapter is a guide on how to trust and obey God as our Father as the biblical prophets did, giving Abraham as one example. We will receive only what we believe God for, whether small or large. The chapter reminds us to cast our vision high.

It also teaches us to be open to God's unlimited power and authority. It encourages us to think positive and expect God's best in your life.

CHAPTER 14: TIME IS NEAR—JESUS IS THE KEY

This chapter is a guide on how to prepare for the return of Jesus Christ. Jesus tells us that He is coming soon for His church—born-again believers. The Bible tells us that we must be born again to see the kingdom of God.

The chapter teaches you how to put on the armor of God daily as you wait for His triumphant return, when the trumpet will sound and will be heard throughout the earth as recorded in the Book of Revelation. The Bible tells us that we will meet Jesus in the air: "The Royal Party."

In this chapter you are reminded that *Jesus is the Key to eternal life.* According to the Word of God, *Jesus holds the key to the door that no one can open or shut.*

INTRODUCTION

This book was written to God's people to encourage you to live a godly life with the help of the Holy Spirit as your guide to a successful life in Christ. Through personal experiences and God's guidance, I have learned to lean on and trust God in all circumstances.

Over the course of my life, I have grown closer to Christ and I am still growing as I seek Him daily for direction and strength. Through Christ all things are possible to those who believe in Him. This book will strengthen your Christian walk and lead you into a deeper relationship with Christ. By reading this book and meditating on the Word of God, you will be encouraged and equipped to accomplish your God-given dreams and desires.

You will be taught how to break the enemy's hold in your life. You will discover issues that hinder many of God's people from reaching their full potential and will be shown the path to redeem all that God has for you. *The Key to Eternity* is a guide to developing a closer relationship with God and communicating with Him on a deeper level. You will be empowered to live a godly and successful life as God leads you to life everlasting with Him in eternity.

In *The Key to Eternity* you will discover that Jesus is the Key to spending eternity in heaven by believing in Him and trusting Him to lead your life. Jesus not only opens the door to eternity, but He empowers you to live the abundant life now. This book will encourage, equip, and strengthen you on your journey to the abundant life promised by Christ.

The thief comes only to steal and kill and destroy; I came
that they may have life, and have it abundantly.
—JOHN 10:10

In this book you will discover fourteen keys that will guide
you to living the abundant life that is promised to you:

1. God's plan for your life

2. Deceitful practices that hinder success

3. God's character through the Book of Esther

4. Who is God?

5. How to hear from God

6. The key to a successful life

7. Things you should always remember about the
   schemes of the enemy

8. Words of wisdom in achieving your God-
   ordained goals and dreams

9. Words of encouragement to develop and maintain a godly lifestyle and achieve success

10. Things to do to develop a closer relationship with
    the Father, God

11. Why things happen to us

12. Why God hates doubt in believers

13. God's unlimited power in your life

14. Time is near—Jesus is the key

Chapter 1

KEY ONE: GOD'S PLAN FOR YOUR LIFE

Have you ever asked yourself, Why I am here? What is the purpose of my life? What does the future hold for me? or, How will my life turn out? Everyone at one time or another has asked these questions. One thing we don't realize is that we are all part of God's perfect plan. The Master Creator, God, has a plan for everyone. All you have to do is get in tune with our Lord and Savior, Jesus Christ, and God will reveal His perfect plan to you. God has destined each one of us to accomplish something on earth. You were not placed here by accident. When you follow the perfect will of God, then God can work through you by the power of the Holy Spirit. When you ask Jesus to come into your life, as Romans 10:9 instructs us, only then can God guide you by sending His Holy Spirit. The Holy Spirit guides or directs you to stay in touch with God's perfect will for your life, whether it's concerning your family, friends, relationships, or finances. Whatever you are experiencing, the Holy Spirit will lead you to the answer or God's will concerning that particular situation.

> I will ask the Father, and He will give you another Helper, that He may be with you forever; that is the Spirit of truth, whom the world cannot receive, because it does not see Him or know Him, but you know Him because He abides with you and will be in you.
>
> —JOHN 14:16–17

3

The Holy Spirit is like an ocean and we are the sailboats; if you stay afloat and follow the waves, your destination will be safe. The sail will be smooth, and at the end of your journey will be your reward. The Holy Spirit is the Leader and we are His followers. He is first in command. The Spirit guides you to the perfect will of God. Our Lord is the Alpha and the Omega, the Beginning and the End, the First and the Last. He knows everything past, present, and future. He is the anchor of our soul.

> This hope we have as an anchor of the soul, a hope both sure and steadfast and one which enters within the veil, where Jesus has entered as a forerunner for us, having become a high priest forever according to the order of Melchizedek.
> —HEBREWS 6:19–20

He decides our final destination according to our will and choices made on earth. The perfect will of God is unknown to men, but can be made known when we lay our burdens and concerns on Him. You must surrender to His will and humble yourself to His authority by trusting Him and allowing Him to lead your life.

> Now those who belong to Christ Jesus have crucified the flesh with its passions and desires. If we live by the Spirit, let us also walk by the Spirit.
> —GALATIANS 5:24–25

> Therefore, brothers and sisters, we have an obligation—but it is not to the flesh, to live according to it. For if you live according to the flesh, you will die; but if by the Spirit you put to death the misdeeds of the body, you will live. For those who are led by the Spirit of God are the children of God. The Spirit you received does not make you slaves, so that you live in fear again; rather, the Spirit you received

brought about your adoption to sonship. And by him we cry, "Abba, Father." The Spirit himself testifies with our spirit that we are God's children. Now if we are children, then we are heirs—heirs of God and co-heirs with Christ, if indeed we share in his sufferings in order that we may also share in his glory.

—ROMANS 8:12–17, NIV

Our heavenly Father knows life is hard, and we make it hard for ourselves because we open the door (called sin) for Satan to bring havoc into our lives. God sent His only begotten Son, Jesus, to come and ease our burdens and to destroy Satan's hold on our lives. Matthew 11:28–30 says, "Come to me, all you who are weary and burdened, and I will give you rest. Take my yoke upon you and learn from me, for I am gentle and humble in heart, and you will find rest for your souls. For my yoke is easy and my burden is light" (NIV). Life becomes more enjoyable as we get closer to God and understand His will for us.

When we are obedient to His will, then He guides us to do many things through Him. Jesus is our Savior; He saved us from ruin, from eternal judgment, pain, and suffering on earth, and from God's wrath that is to come. First Thessalonians 1:10 says, "Wait for His Son from heaven, whom He raised from the dead, that is Jesus, who rescues us from the wrath to come." This was God's last attempt to save His people. God loves us enough to bring us back to Him by His extreme sacrifice of allowing Jesus to take our place on the cross. Our lives can be made perfect when we surrender to God's will, perfect in God's eyes.

The choices we make on earth will determine our final destination after this life, whether it will be with God forever or a place unplanned for us. You make the decision to follow His will or your own will. The Lord is omnipresent and omnipotent. He knows everything, every thought; it is impossible to outthink or outdo God. We would not succeed if we tried.

> There is no wisdom, no insight, no plan that can succeed against the LORD.
>
> —PROVERBS 21:30, NIV

Life can be made more enjoyable when we surrender all authority to Jesus by yielding to His will. We must surrender our children, spouses, and all material possessions to Him. The things we possess on earth are temporary. We cannot take them with us after this life. God has blessed us with these things. That is why we must be good stewards of everything He has given us. Whatever you lose in this world because of God, you will have abundantly in heaven. In Luke 18:22, a man asked Jesus what he must do to inherit eternal life:

> When Jesus heard this, He said to him, "One thing you still lack; sell all that you possess and distribute it to the poor, and you shall have treasure in heaven; and come, follow me."

This passage shows us that to follow Jesus requires surrendering all to God. This passage is not telling you to sell all that you have and give to the poor. Jesus was demonstrating this man's lack of willingness and obedience to surrender everything to Him. Living for Jesus means being willing and obedient to do the things Jesus asks of us. Jesus knew this man treasured his possessions more than the things of God. Jesus has blessed us with the things we have. Everything on earth belongs to God. We must realize that everything we own also belongs to God. God wants us to be a blessing to others.

God desires us to prosper in everything we do: in relationships, in finances, and in health. "Beloved, I pray that in all respects you may prosper and be in good health, just as your soul prospers" (3 John 1:2). God blesses us so we can be a blessing to others. We have to be willing to give to others and not be afraid when we give. When you give or help others, God will give your more than what you gave. Luke 6:38 says, "Give, and it will be given to you. They will pour into your lap a good measure—pressed down, shaken together, and running over. For by your standard of measure it will be measured to you in return." Matthew 25:40 tells us that whatever good you did to another on earth, is like you did it to Jesus himself (author's paraphrase).

> Whatever you do, do your work heartily, as for the Lord rather than for men, knowing that from the Lord you will receive the reward of the inheritance. It is the Lord Christ whom you serve. For he who does wrong will receive the consequences of the wrong which he has done, and that without partiality.
> —COLOSSIANS 3:23–25

Life is a meeting place for saints, to prepare us for what is to come: something unthought-of, not recognizable by human eyes; something immeasurable, indescribable, unimaginable, but real.

Chapter 2

KEY TWO: DECEITFUL PRACTICES

Many people today lead lives of adultery, lust, lying, conjuring of spirits, impatience, idolatry, contempt, and mockery. These desires cannot satisfy the heart. These only draw us away from God. They lead to a life of corruption, confusion, resentment, pain, and hardship. These behaviors are ungodly because they go against the Word of God. Everything we do should be to please our Lord and Savior, not only at home but also on our jobs and everywhere we go.

We should have compassion for others by showing kindness. Hebrews 13:1–2 says, "Let love of the brethren continue. Do not neglect to show hospitality to strangers, for by this some have entertained angels without knowing it." We should treat others with dignity and respect, regardless of their background, social status, or the "cliques" they belong to. Many of us only associate with a particular group of people, thus limiting the opportunity to make a difference in someone's life.

> Be of the same mind toward one another; do not be haughty in mind, but associate with the lowly. Do not be wise in your own estimation. Never pay back evil for evil to anyone, Respect what is right in the sight of all men. If possible, so far as it depends on you, be at peace with all men. Never take your own revenge, beloved, but leave room for the wrath of God, for it is written, "VENGEANCE IS MINE, I WILL REPAY," says the Lord. "BUT IF YOUR ENEMY IS

HUNGRY, FEED HIM, AND IF HE IS THIRSTY, GIVE
HIM A DRINK; FOR IN SO DOING YOU WILL HEAP
BURNING COALS ON HIS HEAD." Do not be overcome
by evil, but overcome evil with good.
—ROMANS 12:16–21

We should treat others like we want to be treated. What is
inside your heart is seen by your actions and emotions; there
should only be goodness towards others in your heart.

Let no unwholesome word proceed from your mouth, but
only such a word as is good for edification according to the
need of the moment, so that it will give grace to those who
hear. Do not grieve the Holy Spirit of God, by whom you
were sealed for the day of redemption. Let all bitterness
and wrath and anger and clamor and slander be put away
from you, along with all malice. Be kind to one another,
tender-hearted, forgiving each other, just as God in Christ
also has forgiven you.
—EPHESIANS 4:29–32

Our lifestyles and behaviors reveal who and what we are. We
teach our children these practices and sometimes we do not
realize that the things we do indeed affect our children's future.

Some of us think we are hiding these things from others, so
we do what pleases us, not knowing the long-term effects these
ungodly relationships or actions will have on our children or the
next generation. These practices will follow us and our children
forever, unless we put a stop to them with the help of Jesus Christ.

When you repent of ungodly practices and ask Jesus into your
life, He will help you to overcome these strongholds. Jesus will
send you the Holy Spirit to help you to resist these sinful temptations. "You are from God, little children, and have overcome
them; because greater is He who is in you than he [Satan] who

is in the world" (1 John 4:4). You are to rebuke Satan when he tempts you to sin, by using the sword of the Spirit, which is the Word of God in the name of Jesus Christ.

People often think that what they do in the dark will never be revealed in the light; but they fail to realize that the light is always on, and He is called Jesus—knowing and seeing all.

> Do not participate in the unfruitful deeds of darkness, but instead even expose them; for it is disgraceful even to speak of the things which are done by them in secret. But all things become visible when they are exposed by the light, for everything that becomes visible is light.
>
> —EPHESIANS 5:11–13

We do not see the spiritual consequences of our actions. These practices only open a door for Satan to cause destruction in our lives, without us even realizing it. These ungodly practices only lead to lives of destruction, confusion, and pain from one generation to another if left unresolved (by not repenting and turning to Christ). We will reap what we sow.

> Either make the tree good and its fruit good or make the tree bad and its fruit bad; for the tree is known by its fruit. You brood of vipers, how can you, being evil, speak what is good? For the mouth speaks out of that which fills the heart. The good man brings out of his good treasure what is good; and the evil man brings out of his evil treasure what is evil. But I tell you that every careless word that people speak, they shall give an accounting for it in the day of judgment. For by your words you will be justified, and by your words you will be condemned.
>
> —MATTHEW 12:33–37

> To sum up, all of you be harmonious, sympathetic, brotherly, kindhearted, and humble in spirit; not returning evil for evil or insult for insult, but giving a blessing instead; for you were called for the very purpose that you might inherit a blessing. For, "The one who desires life, to love and see good days, must keep his tongue from evil and his lips from speaking deceit. He must turn away from evil and do good; he must seek peace and pursue it. For the eyes of the Lord are toward the righteous, and his ears attend to their prayer but the face of the Lord is against those who do evil."
>
> —1 PETER 3:8–12

These ungodly practices tie God's hand of protection over us, thus opening the door for Satan to enter our homes. The Bible tells us that Satan comes to steal, kill, and destroy. He brings sickness, death, and destruction into our lives, but only if we allow him to.

> The thief comes only to steal and kill and destroy; I came that they may have life, and have it abundantly. I am the good shepherd; the good shepherd lays down His life for the sheep.
>
> —JOHN 10:10–11

Because God is holy, we leave His umbrella of protection when we choose to practice ungodliness. When we choose to step out of His will, we are led into a different plan or direction that God did not intend for us. In other words, you walk away from your divine destiny.

> However, you are not in the flesh but in the Spirit, if indeed the Spirit of God dwells in you. But if anyone does not have the Spirit of Christ, he does not belong to Him. If Christ is in you, though the body is dead because of sin, yet the spirit is alive because of righteousness. But if the Spirit of

Him who raised Jesus from the dead dwells in you, He who raised Christ Jesus from the dead will also give life to your mortal bodies through His Spirit who dwells in you. So then, brethren, we are under obligation, not to the flesh, to live according to the flesh—for if you are living according to the flesh, you must die; but if by the Spirit you are putting to death the deeds of the body, you will live. For all who are being led by the Spirit of God, these are sons of God.

—ROMANS 8:9–14

Thanks to Jesus Christ, we can repent by turning from the sin and God will put us back on the road to success, thus fulfilling His plan for our lives. God gives us many chances to live for Him. We serve a forgiving God.

When we rely on other things besides God for happiness, success, and power, we are looking for destruction, failure, and unhappiness.

There is a way which seems right to a man, but its end is the way of death.

—PROVERBS 16:25

Jesus said to him, "I am the way, the truth, and the life; no one comes to the Father but through Me."

—JOHN 14:6

These deceitful practices can never give us true happiness. Happiness that is true and sincere only comes from the Lord. When we repent and ask God for forgiveness, Christ sees our true and sincere hearts and forgives us of every sin we have ever committed, whether large or small. Sin is sin, according to God; sin equals sin.

> Therefore consider the members of your earthly body as dead to immorality, impurity, passion, evil desire, and greed, which amounts to idolatry. For it is because of these things that the wrath of God will come upon the sons of disobedience, and in them you also once walked, when you were living in them. But now you also, put them all aside: anger, wrath, malice, slander, and abusive speech from your mouth. Do not lie to one another, since you laid aside the old self with its evil practices, and have put on the new self who is being renewed to a true knowledge according to the image of the One who created him.
>
> —COLOSSIANS 3:5–10

The Lord desires to lead us away from the strongholds of sin and thoughts that can rule over us, if we allow Him. He wants us to live a life of happiness and peace, which can only come through Him—a life of joy, overflowing joy that we can rest assured will be passed on to our children and our grandchildren. He wants us to prosper in all things. With Him in us we cannot fail. With Him in us we'll never go wrong.

To conjure up spirits is idolatry. To commit adultery is immoral and very unpleasing to God. To lie is an act of ungodliness and should never be practiced. To cheat someone is robbery and leads to a life of corruption. To accept a bribe is unacceptable to the ways of the Lord. "Extortion turns a wise person into a fool, and a bribe corrupts the heart" (Eccles. 7:7, NIV).

> Do you not understand that everything that goes into the mouth passes into the stomach, and is eliminated? But the things that proceed out of the mouth come from the heart, and those defile the man. For out of the heart come evil thoughts, murders, adulteries, fornications, thefts, false witness, slanders. These are the things which defile the man; but to eat with unwashed hands does not defile the man.
>
> —MATTHEW 15:17–20

The character of God is honesty, patience, love, peace, happiness, and last but not least, holiness. He leads us to true happiness—happiness which is indescribable, but real; happiness and peace that surpasses all understanding. Philippians 4:6–7 says, "Do not be anxious about anything, but in every situation, by prayer and petition, with thanksgiving, present your requests to God. And the peace of God, which transcends all understanding, will guard your hearts and your minds in Christ Jesus" (NIV).

The ways of the Lord are perfect and lead to a life of righteousness and favor with Him. Life here on earth is precious to God. He has equipped us with everything we need to survive. Life is a constant battlefield, but the Lord is our shield of protection; when we put Him on and into our hearts and minds, nothing will ever penetrate or disturb our peace that He provides, peace which is perfect.

> You will keep in perfect peace those whose minds are steadfast, because they trust in you.
> —ISAIAH 26:3, NIV

One thing that has changed my life recently that I have learned from God's Word is how to put on the armor of God daily. I had developed a sudden fear of driving in tight, closed-in lanes, the one- or two-lane highways with the cement walls on each side. The lanes were quite narrow because of highway construction. I was afraid that I would hit the vehicle that was beside me. I was especially afraid if I was next to an eighteen-wheeler. These tight lanes often ended after a mile or two and then opened to regular freeway. To drive through this was frightening to me. I would become anxious and I could feel my arms wanting to shake; I felt like I was having a panic attack. I tried not to let anyone notice how I was feeling. I would begin to pray and the feeling would leave, but returned when I drove in that same condition. Then I began to bind the spirit of fear and loose peace around me, in the name of Jesus. I learned to quote 2 Timothy 1:7, "For God has not given us a spirit of fear, but of power and of love and of a sound mind" (NKJV).

One day I was driving to work, and while listening to a Christian radio station I learned how to put on the armor of God. Since then, I began to put on the armor of God daily, and when I did, many things in my life began to change: I no longer have a fear of driving through tight spots. I am more relaxed because the peace of God surrounds me, and certain things that bothered me bother me no more. If I find myself starting to worry about a certain thing or situation that occurred, the armor somehow sustains me—I cannot explain it but my peace is more unbreakable now.

The apostle Paul tells us to put on the full armor of God daily:

> Finally, be strong in the Lord and in the strength of His might. Put on the full armor of God, so that you will be able to stand firm against the schemes of the devil. For our struggle is not against flesh and blood, but against the rulers, against the powers, against the world forces of this darkness, against the spiritual forces of wickedness in the heavenly places. Therefore, take up the full armor of God, so that you will be able to resist in the evil day, and having done everything, to stand firm.
>
> —EPHESIANS 6:10–13

"Submit therefore to God. Resist the devil and he will flee from you" (James 4:7). Submitting to God means submitting to His word. You submit by believing what His Word says and putting it into your heart by meditating on it. So, when you are tempted by the evil one to worry or have fear, you can recall what God's Word says about that particular situation and pray that scripture over your problem. By doing this you are putting your faith into motion by saying the scripture, thus resisting the evil one, causing him to flee from you because you are standing on God's Word. Your faith in God's Word causes the enemy to flee from you. Remember it is not you who makes the enemy flee, but the Word of the almighty God. God's Word has power.

James 2:17 says, "In the same way, faith by itself, if it is not accompanied by action, is dead" (NIV). By quoting the Scripture over yourself or the situation, you are putting your faith to work for you. Isn't that awesome? God has given us everything we need to be overcomers. Praise His Holy name, Jesus!

THE ARMOR OF GOD

Are you dressed for battle today?
Are you ready and guarded with defense scriptures?
Is your mind guarded?
Is your heart guarded?
Do you have your belt on, knowing that Jesus is truth
    and His love surrounds you?
Do you have your shoes of peace on, ready to walk in
    peace today guided by the Holy Spirit?
Are you shielded with the Word of God and the blood
    of Jesus Christ, that no weapon formed against you
    will prosper?
Are you ready to walk in love today, knowing you are
    secure in Christ?

ARMOR OF GOD PRAYER

Say this prayer daily before you start your day and you will see a change in your spirit; you will be more patient, calm, forgiving, and loving:

Lord, I put on the Helmet of Salvation; because I am saved, I have the mind of Christ. My thoughts will be holy and pure today and I will rebuke any thoughts or ideas that will cause me to sin against Thee. I cast down all thoughts and imaginations that exalt themselves against the knowledge of God, and I bring into captivity every thought to the obedience of Christ (2 Corinthians 10:5). I put on the Breastplate of Righteousness; because of Jesus' death on the cross, I am made righteous before You. I surrender my will and my emotions to You today. I will be guided by the Holy Spirit and I will not act out in the flesh or do as the flesh desires but as You direct me today. I put on the Shield of Faith, which reminds me that I am protected and covered by the blood of Jesus Christ and no harm will come to me today, and the temptation to sin will not overcome me, but I will overcome it. I put on the Sword of the Spirit, which is the Word of God. I will use God's words and not my own to ward off the temptations of the evil one, so I will not sin against You today. I put on the Belt of Truth that reminds me that Jesus is truth and His love surrounds me today, and I am to walk in love with others in obedience to You, knowing I am secure in Christ. I put on the Shoes of Peace that You will keep me in perfect peace, and I am to walk in peace with others today, in obedience to You. Thank You, Lord, that You are directing my steps today. I put on the full armor of God today in Jesus' name. Amen.

My friend, you have just prepared yourself to be victorious over your day.

Chapter 3

KEY THREE: THE BOOK OF ESTHER REVEALS GOD'S CHARACTER

In the Book of Esther, the king dethroned Vashti, his queen, because of her disobedience and disrespect to him, and gave her crown to Esther. The king chose Esther over all the other women because of her obedience to him and because of God's favor upon her. The king in the Book of Esther represents God, and Esther represents Christians who are obedient to God. Blessings and God's favor are given to the obedient one in Christ Jesus to fulfill the call of God on his or her life. Esther was born to deliver the Jews from the destruction that was planned for them.

> For to a person who is good in His sight He has given wisdom and knowledge and joy, while to the sinner He has given the task of gathering and collecting so that he may give to one who is good in God's sight. This too is vanity and striving after wind.
> —ECCLESIASTES 2:26

Matthew 21:43 says, "Therefore I say to you, the kingdom of God will be taken away from you and given to a people, producing the fruit of it." This is also seen in the Book of 1 Samuel, where God removes Saul as king because of Saul's disobedience to God, and makes David the new king over Israel.

Esther pleased the king to the point where he gave her anything that her heart desired. This is what God does for us according to Matthew 6:33: "But seek first His kingdom and His righteousness, and all these things will be added to you." Obedience to God and His Word opens the door for God to bless you. When you become born again and allow Jesus to lead your life, God blesses you with peace and daily blessings. As you grow in Christ, you must continue to nourish your spirit with the Word of God on a daily basis. The spirit lies dormant without constant nourishment from God's Holy Book.

Esther fasted and prayed for God's favor and guidance concerning her enemies. Because of her loyalty to the king, he made her enemies her footstool. Everything that her enemies planned for her and the Jews were indeed plans for themselves.

> For David himself says in the book of Psalms, "the lord said to my lord, 'sit at my right hand, until I make your enemies a footstool for your feet.'"
>
> —LUKE 20:42–43

Luke tells us that the plans of our enemy will fail. Whatever our enemy does against us will end up in favor for us; God will use it to elevate us. Isaiah 54:17 says, "'No weapon that is formed against you will prosper; and every tongue that accuses you in judgment you will condemn. This is the heritage of the servants of the LORD, and their vindication is from Me,' declares the LORD." He who favors the Lord will prosper and lead others to Christ.

Esther not only saved herself and Mordecai, but all the Jews from India to Cush. The king provided a yearly Jewish celebration in remembrance of the Jews' triumph over everyone who hated them. They celebrated by giving gifts to the poor, holding days of feasting, and giving presents of food. We do the same thing at Christmas, by celebrating the birth of our Lord Jesus

Christ because He came to free the world of sin by dying on the cross, thus breaking Satan's hold in our lives. Jesus broke the hold of poverty, disease, addiction, and every stronghold brought on by Satan. He freed us forever. All we have to do is believe and take a stand against the strongholds by quoting God's Word over our illness, addiction, or whatever the situation may be. Nothing is too hard for our God to handle. In the name of Jesus you can bind the stronghold and loose God's blessing and/or healing in your life. For example, if your problem is sickness, such as diabetes, say, "The Word of God says in Matthew 16:19, 'I will give you the keys of the kingdom of heaven; whatever you bind on earth will be bound in heaven, and whatever you loose on earth will be loosed in heaven' (NIV). I bind the spirit of infirmity in the name of Jesus Christ, and I loose health and healing over my body in Jesus' name, amen." Do the same for addictions, lack, and poverty.

Whatever your problem may be, because Jesus died for your healing, through Him you can live the abundant life by walking in obedience to His Word. Remember you have to be born again (saved) to speak healing over your problem by confessing that Jesus died on the cross for your sins and that He is Lord. Jesus died so you can have authority over illness and poverty and everything else that comes against you to stop you from living the abundant life in Christ.

Chapter 4

KEY FOUR: WHO IS GOD?

God is a figure of a person unseen by anyone except the Son. "All things have been handed over to Me by My Father, and no one knows who the Son is except the Father, and who the Father is except the Son, and anyone to whom the Son wills to reveal Him" (Luke 10:22). First John 4:12 says, "No one has seen God at any time; if we love one another, God abides in us, and His love is perfected in us." Many have experienced His presence and many know of His glory. He is more than a man could ever be. He has no weakness. His strengths are beyond measure. He is loving in every way on earth and also in heaven.

> Beloved, let us love one another, for love is from God; and everyone who loves is born of God and knows God. The one who does not love does not know God, for God is love. By this the love of God was manifested in us, that God has sent His only begotten Son into the world so that we might live through Him. In this is love, not that we loved God, but that He loved us and sent His Son to be the propitiation for our sins. Beloved, if God so loved us, we also ought to love one another.
>
> —1 JOHN 4:7–11

His goodness is immeasurable and unexplainable to humans. He is not a person so He tells no lies.

> God is not a man that He should lie, Nor a son of man, that He should repent; Has He said, and will He not do it?

> Or has He spoken, and will He not make it good? Behold,
> I have received a command to bless; When He has blessed,
> then I cannot revoke it.
>
> —NUMBERS 23:19–20

He speaks of goodness, fairness, and honesty. God is real to the hearts that know Him and believe in Him. God is never in a hurry. To Him time is immeasurable. God is real to all the senses. We can smell His presence; He is a sweet fragrance to smell. We can hear His voice, if we sit still and talk to Him. We can taste and see the goodness that He brings us in times of despair. We can always feel His love for us. Psalm 34:8 says, "O taste and see that the LORD is good; How blessed is the man who takes refuge in Him!" When we open our hearts to Jesus, He gives us peace.

God is everywhere and His angels are messengers of God. Everyone has a guardian angel assigned by God. Angels help us here on earth; more so when we are obedient to God. Angels appear when we are faced with disaster or when we are in trouble. They are God's protection for us.

> The angel of the LORD encamps around those who fear
> Him, And delivers them.
>
> —PSALM 34:7, NKJV

There are angels of the night and of the day. They travel with us. They lead us when we are in good standing with God.

> Because you have made the LORD, who is my refuge, Even
> the Most High, your dwelling place, No evil shall befall
> you, Nor shall any plague come near your dwelling; For
> He shall give His angels charge over you, To keep you in all
> your ways. In their hands they shall bear you up, Lest you
> dash your foot against a stone.
>
> —PSALM 91:9–12, NKJV

God reminded me of this scripture after going through something that could have been devastating for my family and me. In July of 2009, my family and I spent a week vacationing in Florida. We made the vacation a time of prayer. I felt like God wanted us to spend time with Him on this vacation because of the busyness of our lives. Every day before starting our day in Destin, we gathered to have Bible study. I was seeking God for His direction for our future and the ministry that He was calling us into.

We returned home on Saturday, and on Sunday night at approximately 11:30 p.m. I went into the bathroom. While standing near the vanity, I felt this overwhelming presence of God. All I could do was cry and kneel in worship. I just praised God and thanked Him. It was unlike anything I have ever experienced. I felt like I was kneeling in the glory of God. All I felt was joy and happiness. When I went back to bed, I told Jerry what had happened, and that I thought Jesus or an angel was in the bathroom.

I fell asleep and I had a vision of three angels leaving my bathroom. They were white figures floating together in a row. They went into my living room. When I saw this vision, I immediately woke up. I don't think it was a dream because it was like a flash before my eyes. I awoke Jerry and told him what I had seen. I told him that was probably why I felt the glory of God in my bathroom. I remember asking Jerry, "Why do you think they were here?" He said, "I do not know, but I thank God they are here with us."

Three days later, my son, Leekus, and two of his close friends, Cody and Paula, were in a terrible car accident. My son's car was the only car involved. His car flipped over and was totaled. The emergency crew was amazed that they were not injured and how they were able to exit the car with only bruises and scratches. When I arrived on the scene, all I could do was pray that they were all right because the car looked horrible. I thanked Jesus for keeping them safe.

After returning home from the emergency room, I remembered the experience that I had in the bathroom and the vision of the angels that occurred only three days prior to the accident. I know without a doubt that God wanted me to see for myself that Psalm 91:9–12 is true. God sent the three angels in advance to protect my son and his two friends. God is awesome and loving in every way. I am so thankful to Him. I thank God for His protection. His Word is true. He sends His angels to protect us. Praise His name! He is the great "I AM." He is everything to us. He is our protector, our provider, our comforter, our way maker, our healer. He is everything we need. He is our Lord!

God is our light to eternal life, an endless beam of radiance. He is forever and His love is everlasting. God is who He says He is in Exodus 3:13–15:

> Then Moses said to God, "Behold, I am going to the sons of Israel, and I will say to them, 'The God of your fathers has sent me to you.' Now they may say to me, 'What is His name?' What shall I say to them?" God said to Moses, "I AM WHO I AM"; and He said, "Thus you shall say to the sons of Israel, 'I AM has sent me to you.'" God, furthermore, said to Moses, "Thus you shall say to the sons of Israel, 'The LORD, the God of your fathers, the God of Abraham, the God of Isaac, and the God of Jacob, has sent me to you.' This is My name forever, and this is My memorial-name to all generations."

Chapter 5

KEY FIVE: HOW TO HEAR FROM GOD

The Spirit of the Lord has spoken to many people as we can see from the Bible. God spoke to Moses through the burning bush to go and get His people out of Egypt. God spoke to Abraham many times, showing him the future of his descendants. God spoke to Mary, the mother of Jesus, through the angel Gabriel.

God speaks to us in many ways, more so when we have a personal relationship with Him. God seeks to have a personal relationship with everyone through His Son, Jesus Christ. The Cross is where the relationship starts, when you come to know Christ as your Lord and Savior. Many come to Jesus because of crossroads in their lives when they discover that they can no longer live without a true purpose; then they surrender to Him. Jesus fills that empty space inside. He makes us whole. He gives us purpose and value. That's where the relationship begins, and it continues to grow as you meditate on the Word of God and spend quality time with Him.

As you begin to spend quality time alone with God, He will begin to speak to you and through you. Many people do not take time to seek God. Hebrews 11:6 says, "But without faith it is impossible to please Him, for he who comes to God must believe that He is, and that He is a rewarder of those who diligently seek Him" (NKJV).

The more you spend time with God, the better you will become at distinguishing His voice. "When he puts forth all his own, he goes ahead of them, and the sheep follow him because they know his voice. A stranger they simply will not follow, but will flee from him, because they do not know the voice of strangers" (John 10:4–5).

When God speaks to you, His words are never condemning or discouraging, and they will never bring guilt or shame. Those are the words of the enemy. God speaks love, patience, and compassion towards us. He does correct our behavior, but in a loving way.

> And you have forgotten the exhortation which is addressed to you as sons, "MY SON, DO NOT REGARD LIGHTLY THE DISCIPLINE OF THE LORD, NOR FAINT WHEN YOU ARE REPROVED BY HIM; FOR THOSE WHOM THE LORD LOVES HE DISCIPLINES, AND HE SCOURGES EVERY SON WHOM HE RECEIVES." It is for discipline that you endure; God deals with you as with sons; for what son is there whom his father does not discipline?
>
> —HEBREWS 12:5-7

The Spirit of God can speak to a person in many different ways: directly from God, through the Holy Spirit, by way of visions and dreams, or by angels that speak to people as God directs. God Himself determines which way He chooses to convey a message to an individual.

God can send a person a message through another individual, also known as a prophet. We see this throughout the New and Old Testaments. Prophets are God's chosen vessels or conduits for information to be delivered to another person. God chooses prophets from birth, such as John the Baptist, Samuel, and Jeremiah, just to name a few.

> Now the word of the LORD came to me saying, "Before I formed you in the womb I knew you, And before you were born I consecrated you; I have appointed you a prophet to the nations." Then I said, "Alas, Lord GOD! Behold, I do not know how to speak, Because I am a youth." But the LORD said to me, "Do not say, 'I am a youth,' Because everywhere I send you, you shall go, And all that I command you, you shall speak. Do not be afraid of them, For I am with you to deliver you," declares the LORD.
>
> —JEREMIAH 1:4–8

Many of them suffered persecution because God used them to inform or correct others, which is usually not popular. But regardless of the popularity of the calling, they did it because of their obedience of God. They obeyed God despite man's reaction to the message or them.

God uses prophets to bring good news as well to others who are obeying Him. An example would be when God sent Samuel the prophet to anoint David as the next king of Israel (1 Sam. 16:13). God can also use a disciple to give a message, as when God sent Ananias, the disciple, to Paul to heal his eyes (Acts 9:10). God uses prophets to give messages to nations to turn the people's heart back to Him, such as Jeremiah, John the Baptist, and Jonah. God's prophets play a major role in conveying God's messages to individuals and nations. That was true in biblical times as well as today. Many people do not believe that God speaks today; therefore, they never hear from Him. Faith is what moves God to speak to you in whatever way He chooses. Faith moves the hand of God; faith pleases God.

> But without faith it is impossible to please Him, for he who comes to God must believe that He is, and that He is a rewarder of those who diligently seek Him.
>
> —HEBREWS 11:6, NKJV

You may ask, what is faith? According to Hebrews 11:1, "Faith is the assurance of things hoped for, the conviction of things not seen." Faith is hope in something and for something that you cannot see. Like God, for instance; you cannot see Him, but by faith you know God exists. For example, Abraham believed God for a son twenty years before he saw the birth of Isaac. Abraham believed before he saw the promise. Abraham is our father of faith.

> Without becoming weak in faith he contemplated his own body, now as good as dead since he was about a hundred years old, and the deadness of Sarah's womb; yet, with respect to the promise of God, he did not waver in unbelief but grew strong in faith, giving glory to God, and being fully assured that what God had promised, He was able also to perform. Therefore IT WAS ALSO CREDITED TO HIM AS RIGHTEOUSNESS.
>
> —ROMANS 4:19–22

Faith is like cooking; you have faith in the fire that it will cook the food. By faith you stir the pot to cook the food. Your faith is getting the skillet, putting oil into it, and then stirring the food. You have faith that as you stir the pot, the fire will thoroughly cook the food. All you have to do is stir the food; waiting, watching, and expecting the food to cook for a good meal. The same applies to the Word of God:

> Truly I say to you, whoever says to this mountain, "Be taken up and cast into the sea," and does not doubt in his heart, but believes that what he says is going to happen, it will be granted him. Therefore I say to you, all things for which you pray and ask, believe that you have received them, and they will be granted you.
>
> —MARK 11:23–24

When you pray and ask God to heal you, save your loved ones, or whatever the Scripture says you have a right to receive because of walking upright before the Lord, it will be granted to you. You have a right to claim the Scripture and believe it will come to pass. Believe God for what you are asking for, such as healing to your body. God's Word says in Isaiah 53:5 that you are healed by Jesus' stripes. His word of *promise* is the *fire*; the *food* is what you are believing God for. You *stir* up your *faith by proclaiming* everyday that your body is healed according to this scripture. By doing this until you see it come to pass, you are *stirring, waiting, watching, and expecting* to see the cooked food (your healing, deliverance, salvation of a loved one, etc.). The Bible tells us that your prayer will be granted. You will see your *"cooked food."* By quoting the scripture and proclaiming your healing to yourself, you will strengthen your faith to believe. The more you say it, the more you will believe. God honors faith.

The problem is that many stop believing if they do not see it instantly. They put out the fire by not quoting the promise. They stop proclaiming it (stirring their faith); they stop waiting and watching and believing to see the finished meal. Many stop believing or participating, and many become bitter. Never stop stirring your faith by quoting the Word of God that you believe for. Never stop watching for your victory. Never stop believing for your miracle.

God can speak to an individual directly. I have heard the thundering voice of God. He can also speak to you through quiet times spent alone with Him. I remember a time when God spoke to me for the first time. It was a quiet voice spoken within my spirit. I was asleep and I was awakened to these words: "Peter did not bite the ear of his listeners." If you can imagine, my eyes popped open, and I began to look around the room. While my husband, Jerry, was asleep, I grabbed his shoulder asking him if he said something to me. He stated that he did not. This occurred several months after I gave my life to Christ. I was seeking God by spending time with Him and reading the Scriptures. Even though the Spirit of God had spoken to me in a parable, I knew exactly what He meant. He was telling me that a teacher of Christ should not accuse the listeners but should teach them without being judgmental.

"Teach in love" is what God was saying; because that is how the disciples and Jesus taught. After this occurred, my faith in God increased because this statement was an answer to a prayer I was seeking Him about. I knew without a doubt that God was real and that He hears our prayers.

I have a few other experiences when the Lord has spoken to me in dreams and in my spirit that I would like to share with you. I share this to bring glory to His name. I was taking classes to further my nursing career. I wanted to become a Naturopathic Doctor. One night I dreamed that I had taken my last class because God was sending me to a Bible college. I awoke from the dream and began to talk to God, not out loud but to myself. I said, "Lord, I thought you were calling me to do natural healing?" The Spirit of the Lord spoke these words to me, not out loud, but within my spirit: "Divine healing." Since then, God has been directing me to have a healing ministry. We have seen many people healed in the name of Jesus Christ.

Another time the Lord gave me a message in a dream to confirm what He was calling me to do. I dreamed that I was teaching people the Word of God, and this lady came up to me and said, "God has called you to minister to His people because you are willing."

Over the past eight to nine years, God has shown me dreams of praying for people and they would be healed. When He told me it was time to start the healing ministry. I felt unqualified. I did not know what to do. So, I began to seek God to teach me what to do in the meetings. I did not know how He would heal people. Then one night, I dreamed that Jesus was telling me to focus on God and not the people in the meetings and that God would do the rest. The first meeting after receiving this message went quite well. I was still unsure of how I was to focus on God. So, I made up my mind that I would do what I was told. I began to praise and worship God and just focus on Jesus and not the people.

While praising Him, God began to give me words of knowledge concerning the people in attendance. I was amazed and so were the people. God wanted me to surrender myself to Him, and He would take over. He would do what I could not. God began to speak to me concerning people that I did not know anything about. He had me tell them things only they knew—information which could only come from God because I knew nothing about them or their personal lives. God also had me call out sickness and diseases that people had and for them to come up for prayer and healing. As they came forward, He told me what that person needed prayer for. God did exactly what He said He would do. All He wanted me to do was to focus on Him and He would do the rest; and He did. God is glorified in our limitations.

I have shared my testimonies with you to encourage you that God will use you also. All you have to do is yield yourself to Him and obey Him. He will do the rest. He will lead you to your divine call; whether it is in business, ministry, sports, music, etc. As you spend time with God, you will learn how to recognize His voice.

He will reveal Himself to you. God desires to fellowship with you. When you are doing what God has called you to do, He will be faithful to help and guide you to accomplish all He has destined for you. Do not worry about what He has called you to do; just seek first His kingdom and His righteousness and He will guide you into your divine call. Praise be to God!

God can also speak to you through His Word. He will lead you to scriptures that will relate to what you are going through during the difficult times. He will lead you to passages that will comfort you and reassure you to continue in faith. He will give you direction concerning your life.

Another way God chooses to communicate to us is by signs and wonders. God and Jesus performed signs and wonders all throughout the Bible. Jesus said in John 10:37–38, "If I do not the works of My Father, do not believe Me; but if I do them, though you do not believe Me, believe the works, so that you may know and understand that the Father is in Me, and I in the Father."

In the Book of Exodus, God told Moses to go and lead His people out of Egypt. God told Moses that the Hebrews would know that God was with him because of the signs and wonders that God would perform through Moses (Exod. 4:1–9). Moses not only had to convince the pharaoh that God was with him, but he had to convince the Hebrews as well with signs from God.

Sometimes despite the evidence of God's existence and power, some still refuse to believe. That is what happened to Christ. The Sadducees and Pharisees could not see that Jesus was the Christ despite the overwhelming evidence of miracles they saw first-hand. When Jesus cast out demons from people, the Pharisees accused Him of being demon possessed. Jesus answered them and said that Satan could not cast out Satan (Matt. 12:22–27). Jesus is the healer; Satan is the one that causes sickness. Unfortunately, many people still feel that way today, despite the overwhelming evidence that Jesus heals (Isa. 53:5).

Another sign and wonder that God uses to demonstrate His power is through the Holy Spirit. The Holy Spirit sets us free from the bondage of sin. Many people, when they come to know our Lord and Savior Jesus Christ, are able to be set free from addictions such as alcoholism, pornography, criminal activity, lying, and all other bondages of Satan by the power of the Holy Spirit working within them.

One miraculous sign of God is when He touches a person to surrender his or her life to Jesus by making him or her born again. John 3:3 says, "Jesus answered and said to him, 'Truly, truly, I say to you, unless one is born again he cannot see the kingdom of God.'" Being born again is an amazing miracle.

God also communicates to us by the manifestations of the Holy Spirit. You cannot see the Holy Spirit, but you can definitely feel His presence when He manifests Himself to you. God uses the Holy Spirit to communicate to us, which is that still quiet voice that whispers to our inner soul. The Holy Spirit is our guide. The Holy Spirit is our teacher.

> But, the Helper, the Holy Spirit, whom the Father will send in My name, He will teach you all things, and bring to your remembrance all that I said to you.
> —JOHN 14:26

The Holy Spirit also intercedes to God on our behalf by the power of speaking in tongues. "So then tongues are for a sign, not to those who believe but to unbelievers; but prophecy is for a sign, not to unbelievers but to those who believe" (1 Cor. 14:22). The Holy Spirit prays to God for us, things that we do not know how and what to pray for.

One of the most important ways that we hear from God is by praying and fasting. When we sacrifice something, whether it is food or something else that we give up while spending time in prayer before God, I believe that moves God. In my personal experiences, when I needed to hear from God, I fasted for a period of time. I usually will fast food, and God has never failed to answer my prayer after fasting, or to direct me in the path in which I should go. He is always faithful. There are many different types of fasting you can read about in books and on the Internet. I know from personal experiences that God honors praying and fasting.

Many people hear from God during their "burning bush" experience. A "burning bush" is an obstacle that God wants to bring you out of. It can also be during wondering times, when people are searching for their identity and purpose in life. When you are seeking God for answers is when He reveals Himself to you. Many times it is when your "bush is burning." Moses tried to help the Hebrew slaves from the bondage of Pharaoh in his own strength, but he failed. After he realized he could not accomplish this on his own, he set out to find his purpose. Moses had to surrender the desire to help the Hebrews to God. That's when God revealed Himself to Moses in the burning bush and empowered him to free the Hebrews.

Beloved, we need the power of God to be set free and to overcome obstacles we cannot accomplish on our own. Just as Moses needed the power of the almighty God to guide him in leading the Hebrews out of bondage, we need God's power as well in our lives. That is the power of the Holy Spirit that resides within you after you receive Christ as your Lord and Savior. Many of us have problems in our lives that we want to be free from, but it is not until we surrender the problem, addiction, sickness, etc., over to God that He will help us to overcome our obstacles and set us free by the power of His Holy Spirit.

Another time God revealed to me that He was taking my relative home to be with Him. This relative was very sick and had been for a long time. I remember praying to God asking Him to reveal to me when He was getting ready to take my relative home, because I wanted to see her again before she left this earth. The Spirit of the Lord told me within my spirit (not audibly) while asleep, to go and pray for my relative and anoint her with oil and she would recover. As the Spirit of the Lord told me this, I saw a vision of this scripture:

> Is anyone among you sick? Then he must call for the elders of the church and they are to pray over him, anointing him with oil in the name of the Lord; and the prayer offered in faith will restore the one who is sick, and the Lord will raise him up, and if he has committed sins, they will be forgiven him.
>
> —JAMES 5:14–15

I was obedient and did as God said. Four days after praying, around 12:00 a.m., I dreamed that I visited my relative and she was awake and quite alert. She was talking to everyone and watching television while sitting up. One of her daughters was embracing her. Her entire family and all her relatives were in the room. She was very happy. She was no longer sick. I talked to her and she talked to me. She and I began to praise and thank God for healing her. This is what I dreamed. I awoke and thanked God for healing my relative and I wrote the dream down so I could remember it.

Well, one day around 11:30, I called my mother for our daily ministry prayer, where we pray for the prayers that come to us from the website. I began to tell her of the dream I had during the night, and we began to thank God for showing us in this dream that my relative was going to be healed. Later that same day I found out that my relative went to be with the Lord.

> We are of good courage, I say, and prefer rather to be absent from the body and to at home with the Lord.
>
> —2 CORINTHIANS 5:8

> For to me, to live is Christ and to die is gain. But if I am to live on in the flesh, this will mean fruitful labor for me;

and I do not know which to choose. But I am hard-pressed
from both directions, having the desire to depart and be
with Christ, for that is very much better.

—PHILIPPIANS 1:21–23

I knew without a doubt that God was showing me the He was
taking my relative home and that she would no longer be sick.
God, however, did answer our prayers of healing her by taking
her with Him. I thank God that she is healed, happy, and celebrating victory with Him.

We have to pray prayers of faith and trust God with the outcome. If you are praying for a person and believing God to heal
him or her, do not get discouraged if you do not see the healing on
earth. If you are saved, your prayers will be answered. When you
go to be with the Lord or if Jesus comes before you die and you
get raptured into heaven, God will show Himself faithful to your
prayer. You will see your loved one healthy and whole in heaven.

But we do not want you to be uninformed, brethren, about
those who are asleep, so that you will not grieve as do the
rest who have no hope. For if we believe that Jesus died
and rose again, even so God will bring with Him those
who have fallen asleep in Jesus. For this we say to you by
the word of the Lord, that we who are alive and remain
until the coming of the Lord, will not precede those who
have fallen asleep. For the Lord Himself will descend from
heaven with a shout, with the voice of the archangel and
with the trumpet of God, and the dead in Christ will rise
first. Then we who are alive and remain will be caught up
together with them in the clouds to meet the Lord in the
air, and so we shall always be with the Lord. Therefore
comfort one another with these words.

—1 THESSALONIANS 4:13–18

Remember that faith is the assurance of things hoped for and the evidence of things not seen (Heb. 11:1). Just because you did not see the loved one healthy and whole on earth, does not mean He did not do it. I believed that God would heal my relative on earth, but He chose to heal her by taking her with Him. That is the ultimate healing. Being with Christ—can you imagine being in His glory! I believe I will see my relative happy and whole just as I saw in the dream.

I had another experience when God revealed to me in a dream when He would come for my sister, Kim. She was diagnosed with cervical cancer and had a hysterectomy. Her doctor reported no further cancer; little did we know, the cancer had metastasized a short period of time after the operation. We prayed to God for her and we expected a physical healing. One night the Lord revealed to me in a dream that Kim would be healed. In this dream I saw her standing in the center of her hospital room; she was dancing around the room saying she was healed. While she danced I noticed that her room was decorated for a celebration. It was like she was healed on someone's birthday. We were celebrating something, and at the same time she was healed. That's what I dreamed.

Kim went to be with the Lord on Resurrection Sunday. God was revealing to me that He would take her home to be with Him on a special day; a day of celebrating the death and resurrection of our Lord and Savior, Jesus Christ. She died on a wonderful day, and we know we will see her again because that is the hope we have in Jesus Christ. That's the purpose of the Cross, eternal life. We will praise God together in His glory.

But that the dead are raised, even Moses showed, in the passage about the burning bush, where he calls the Lord THE GOD OF ABRAHAM, AND THE GOD OF ISAAC,

AND THE GOD OF JACOB. Now He is not the God of the
dead but of the living; for all live to Him.

—LUKE 20:37–38

I have shared these experiences with you to bring glory to the
Father. He will speak to you and will reveal things to you to comfort you and to let you know that He is with you always during
the good times as well as the times of uncertainty. Whatever way
God chooses to speak to you, prepare yourself to hear from Him
by spending time with Him. Pray for discernment of the things
that He will reveal to you.

Chapter 6

KEY SIX: THE KEY TO A SUCCESSFUL LIFE

Success has a different meaning to each person. For one person success may mean being financially secure. To another it means having a good corporate or high-standing job. To another it means having plenty of power to rule. The true meaning of success, as far as God is concerned, is having a devoted relationship with Him by allowing God to communicate to you. Romans 8:31 says, "What then shall we say to these things? If God is for us, who is against us?" Successful living, financial blessings, a peaceful soul, and a sound mind are what you receive when you submit to God's authority in your life. We are successful when we allow God to lead our lives.

Success is not whom we know or how many people we know, nor how much money we have in our bank accounts; success is what God says about you. Are you a man or a woman who can be trusted? Are you a person with honor, dignity, and integrity, or a person whom we would never tell anything to because of fear of gossip, greed, or belittlement? What kind of person are you? The kind of person we are determines our success, not only in the world but also in Christ. Many of us today believe in change, but few of us actually change or are willing to give up beliefs and behaviors that go against the Word of God for Christ's sake and for the benefit of our families, friends, and for ourselves.

Many feel that they would have to give up too much and nothing or no one is worth that. We don't realize that Jesus gave up His life for us so we can have life on earth and have it more abundantly. "The thief comes only to steal and kill and destroy; I came that they may have life, and have it abundantly" (John 10:10). It is time for God's people to start living the abundant life in Christ Jesus.

What we give up on earth can never compare to what Jesus gave up for us. He did this so we could live in peace on earth. So we could escape God's wrath. "But God demonstrates His own love toward us, in that while we were yet sinners, Christ died for us. Much more then, having now been justified by His blood, we shall be saved from the wrath of God through Him" (Rom. 5:8–9). He came to earth so we could reap God's blessings on earth by giving up His life on the cross, He gave us access to God. Christ, who knew no sin, died because of our sin. He died on our behalf. His blood washes us clean of all sin when we acknowledge Him and repent. We are made righteous through Christ. That is why we have a right to approach God's throne and receive answers to our prayers and be healed of all diseases and disorders, including depression. God does not see us with our sin, but He sees His son, Jesus, instead.

Jesus was the perfect Lamb God needed to make atonement for the sin of man. He was the perfect sacrifice. God did not force Jesus to give up His life. Jesus did it because He loved us so much. Jesus could have called a thousand angels to rescue Him, but He didn't. You are so precious to God that He sent his only begotten Son. "For God so loved the world, that He gave His only begotten Son, that whoever believes in Him shall not perish, but have eternal life" (John 3:16). We could not go to God in our sin. So Jesus stood and took our sin and infirmities and placed them on the cross, thus releasing the world of the bondage of sin and Satan. He made us free!

He died so we could overcome Satan and his schemes. God provided a way of escape; we no longer have to submit to sickness and disease, sickness and disease have to submit to us in the name of Jesus Christ. Many people choose to remain bound to sickness, grief, addictions, and self-gratifying behaviors not knowing that Jesus freed us from these things.

> These things I have spoken to you, so that in Me you may have peace. In the world you have tribulation, but take courage; I have overcome the world.
>
> —JOHN 16:33

It is our decision and will that keeps us from experiencing and receiving all that Jesus has for us. We were healed when Jesus died on the cross. He paid our debt in full. We are no longer bound to sin and sickness. We are free!

We don't realize that all we have to do and all God wants us to do is rid ourselves of ungodly practices and behaviors in the name of Jesus Christ by the power of the Holy Spirit. It is only in the name of Jesus that healing is given. We have no power within ourselves other than the Holy Spirit to heal, deliver, and bring salvation. Acts 1:8 says, "But you will receive power when the Holy Spirit has come upon you; and you shall be witnesses to Me in Jerusalem, and in all Judea and Samaria, and to the end of the earth."

Believe with all your heart that these practices will come to an end in your life. Allow yourself to change as God makes the changes in your life. Always remember that God is at your side helping you through this. Believe in Him. Seek Him out and He will make His presence known to you.

> So I say to you, ask, and it will be given to you; seek, and you will find; knock, and it will be opened to you. For

> everyone who asks, receives; and he who seeks, finds; and
> to him who knocks, it will be opened.
>
> —Luke 11:9–10, nkjv

God is always with us. We obey a patient God. He waits for us to make that crucial decision to allow Him to rule over our lives. Call upon Jesus, today!

Many people wait for something crucial or devastating to happen to them before deciding to call on Jesus for help. Don't wait! Call on Him right now! He is waiting for your call. Romans 10:9 tells us, "If you confess with your mouth Jesus as Lord, and believe in your heart that God raised Him from the dead, you will be saved." Ask Jesus into your heart right now by saying this prayer:

> *Jesus, I believe you are my Lord and Savior. You died on the cross for me, for the forgiveness of my sins. Reside in me right now and lead me to do Your will and not my own. Take charge of my life. I yield it to You. Forgive me of every sin. I thank You for Your forgiveness. You are my Lord and Savior; I love You with all my heart. Amen.*

If you said this prayer and believe what this verse tells you, then Jesus resides in you now. The Spirit of God now lives in you. Your body is the temple of God. You are saved! Your name is written in heaven; rejoice, because the Bible tells us that when one person is saved the angels are rejoicing in heaven: "In the same way, I tell you, there is joy in the presence of the angels of God over one sinner who repents" (Luke 15:10). Begin to read the Bible daily. As you read the Bible and meditate on what God is saying, He will reveal many things to you through His Word. God will give you understanding and interpretation, so you can use and apply Scripture in your life. The Bible is a guide to living right before God.

The Bible is the key to living a successful life. Find a Bible that is easily understood and join a Bible-teaching church if you are not currently in one where you will be taught the Word of God and be encouraged as you fellowship with other believers. The Bible tells us it is important to assemble with other believers: "And let us consider how to stimulate one another to love and good deeds, not forsaking our own assembling together, as is the habit of some, but encouraging one another; and all the more as you see the day drawing near" (Heb. 10:24–25). Remember that salvation is not about religion, but having a personal relationship with Jesus Christ.

The Lord will guide you and teach you how to rebuke the temptation to sin in the name of Jesus Christ, and God will strengthen you to overcome sinful desires. Stay focused on God by using His Word against the enemy's attacks. We fight evil with the Word of God, not by our own strength. "For though we walk in the flesh, we do not war according to the flesh, for the weapons of our warfare are not of the flesh, but divinely powerful for the destruction of fortresses" (2 Cor. 10:3–4). God's words have much power over the enemy and over sin and temptations to sin.

When Satan tells you, "You can not overcome the addiction," or "You are not healed," quote healing scriptures. Jesus died in order to give us eternal life in heaven with God, and healing to our bodies. Confess your healing every day with confidence, out loud to yourself, even if you do not see the healing manifested yet. Find out what God says about your particular situation in the Bible and claim the promise for yourself. Find the scripture that applies to your situation and speak it out loud over yourself; that's putting your faith into action. Then expect God to move on your behalf. God will honor your faith in Him.

So faith comes from hearing, and hearing by the word of Christ.

—ROMANS 10:17

But He was wounded for our transgressions, He was bruised for our iniquities; The chastisement for our peace was upon Him, And by His stripes we are healed.

—ISAIAH 53:5, NKJV

Here are a few of God's promises for you. Find the one or as many as you are in need of, and lay claim to them. I have gathered many of God's promises on 3x5 index cards, bound together. I pray them out loud daily and I thank God and claim each one. So, when I start my day, if I am tempted to have fear, worry, doubt, or if my peace is threatened, I recall the scripture and speak it over myself until my joy and peace return.

At one time I carried them with me in my purse, but now many are in my heart. I use them as my emergency rescue scriptures. If the one you need is not here, go to the Bible, write it down, and carry it with you wherever you go. Speak it to yourself until the promise is manifested. Don't be discouraged when you do this because the enemy will try to get you to doubt the promise; remember—that's his job. Tell Satan he is a liar and a thief. Stay encouraged; get around positive people who will encourage you as well. The Bible tells us to "resist the devil and he will flee" (James 4:7). Rebuke Satan with the Word of God, and speak your promise loudly and as often as you need to, until the enemy flees (until you sense God's peace around you). God's promises are alive and real!

Not one of the good promises which the LORD had made to the house of Israel failed; all came to pass.

—JOSHUA 21:45

Let us hold fast the confession of our hope without wavering, for He who promised is faithful.

—HEBREWS 10:23

For all the promises of God in Him are Yes, and in Him Amen, to the glory of God through us.

—2 CORINTHIANS 1:20, NKJV

GOD'S PROMISES TO PRAY TO RESIST FEAR

For God has not given us a spirit of fear, but of power and of love and of a sound mind.

—2 TIMOTHY 1:7, NKJV

Because you have made the LORD, who is my refuge, Even the Most High, your dwelling place, No evil shall befall you, Nor shall any plague come near your dwelling; For He shall give His angels charge over you, To keep you in all your ways. In their hands they shall bear you up, Lest you dash your foot against a stone.

—PSALM 91:9–12, NKJV

And I will give you the keys of the kingdom of heaven, and whatever you bind on earth will be bound in heaven, and whatever you loose on earth will be loosed in heaven.

—MATTHEW 16:19, NKJV

I will both lie down in peace, and sleep; For you alone, O LORD, make me dwell in safety.

—PSALM 4:8, NKJV

"No weapon formed against you shall prosper, And every tongue which rises against you in judgment You shall condemn. This is the heritage of the servants of the LORD, and their righteousness is from Me," Says the LORD.

—ISAIAH 54:17, NKJV

The name of the LORD is a strong tower; The righteous run to it and are safe.

—PROVERBS 18:10, NKJV

Behold, I give you the authority to trample on serpents and scorpions, and over all the power of the enemy, and nothing shall by any means hurt you.

—LUKE 10:19, NKJV

When you pass through the waters, I will be with you; And through the rivers, they shall not overflow you. When you walk through the fire, you shall not be burned, Nor shall the flame scorch you.

—ISAIAH 43:2, NKJV

Yea, though I walk through the valley of the shadow of death, I will fear no evil; For You are with me; Your rod and Your staff, they comfort me.

—PSALM 23:4, NKJV

He who dwells in the secret place of the Most High Shall abide under the shadow of the Almighty. I will say of the LORD, "He is my refuge and my fortress; My God, in Him I will trust."

—PSALM 91:1–2, NKJV

I will lift up my eyes to the hills—From whence comes my help? My Help comes from the LORD, Who made heaven and earth. He will not allow your foot to be moved; He who keeps you will not slumber. Behold, He who keeps Israel Shall neither slumber nor sleep.

—PSALM 121:1–4, NKJV

The LORD is your keeper; The LORD is your shade at your right hand. The sun shall not strike you by day, Nor the moon by night. The LORD shall preserve you from all evil; He shall preserve your soul. The LORD shall preserve your going out and your coming in From this time forth, and even forevermore.

—PSALM 121:5–8, NKJV

He stores up sound wisdom for the upright; He is a shield to those who walk uprightly; He guards the paths of justice, And preserves the way of His saints.

—PROVERBS 2:7–8, NKJV

So we boldly say: "The LORD is my helper; I will not fear. What can man do to me?"

—HEBREWS 13:6, NKJV

But whoever listens to me will dwell safely, And will be secure, without fear of evil.

—PROVERBS 1:33, NKJV

You will not be afraid of the terror by night, Nor of the arrow that flies by day, Nor of the pestilence that walks in darkness, Nor of the destruction that lays waste at noonday. A thousand may fall at your side, And ten thousand at your right hand; But it shall not come near you.

—PSALM 91:5–7, NKJV

The LORD also will roar from Zion, And utter His voice from Jerusalem; The heavens and earth will shake; But the LORD will be a shelter for His people, And the strength of the children of Israel.

—JOEL 3:16, NKJV

The LORD gave them rest all around, according to all that He had sworn to their fathers. And not a man of all their

enemies stood against them; the LORD delivered all their
enemies into their hand. Not a word failed of any good
thing which the LORD had spoken to the house of Israel.
All came to pass.

—JOSHUA 21:44–45, NKJV

GOD'S PROMISES TO PRAY TO RESIST WORRYING

But seek first the kingdom of God and His righteousness,
and all these things shall be added to you.

—MATTHEW 6:33, NKJV

Be anxious for nothing, but in everything by prayer and
supplication, with thanksgiving, let your requests be made
known to God; and the peace of God, which surpasses all
understanding, will guard your hearts and minds through
Christ Jesus.

—PHILIPPIANS 4:6–7, NKJV

Trust in the LORD with all your heart, And lean not on
your own understanding; In all your ways acknowledge
Him, And He shall direct your paths.

—PROVERBS 3:5–6, NKJV

And we know that all things to work together for good to
those who love God, to those who are the called according
to His purpose.

—ROMANS 8:28, NKJV

Praise the LORD! Blessed is the man who fears the LORD,
Who delights greatly in His commandments. His descendants will be mighty on earth; The generation of the
upright will be blessed. Wealth and riches will be in his
house, And his righteousness endures forever.

—PSALM 112:1–3, NKJV

The generous soul will be made rich, And he who waters will also be watered himself.

—PROVERBS 11:25, NKJV

He who trusts in his riches will fall, But the righteous will flourish like foliage [green leaf].

—PROVERBS 11:28, NKJV

Evil pursues sinners, But to the righteous, good shall be repaid. A good man leaves an inheritance to his children's children, But the wealth of the sinner is stored up for the righteous.

—PROVERBS 13:21–22, NKJV

The righteous eats to the satisfying of his soul, But the stomach of the wicked shall be in want.

—PROVERBS 13:25, NKJV

Beloved, I pray that you may prosper in all things and be in health, just as you soul prospers.

—3 JOHN 1:2, NKJV

The house of the wicked will be overthrown, But the tent of the upright will flourish.

—PROVERBS 14:11, NKJV

Then the LORD your God will bring you to the land which your fathers possessed, and you shall possess it. He will prosper you and multiply you more than your fathers.

—DEUTERONOMY 30:5, NKJV

Honor the LORD with your possessions, And with the firstfruits of all your increase; So your barns will be filled with plenty, And your vats will overflow with new wine.

—PROVERBS 3:9–10, NKJV

I have been young, and now am old; Yet I have not seen the righteous forsaken, Nor his descendants begging bread. He is ever merciful, and lends; And his descendants are blessed.

—Psalm 37:25–26, nkjv

Praise the Lord! Blessed is the man who fears the Lord, Who delights greatly in His commandments. His descendants will be mighty on earth; The generation of the upright will be blessed. Wealth and riches will be in his house, And his righteousness endures forever.

—Psalm 112:1–3, nkjv

The righteous man walks in his integrity; His children are blessed after him.

—Proverbs 20:7, nkjv

God's Promises to Pray to Resist Doubt

You are of God, little children, and have overcome them, because He who is in you is greater than he who is in the world.

—1 John 4:4, nkjv

What then shall we say to these things? If God is for us, who can be against us?

—Romans 8:31, nkjv

Beat your plowshares into swords, And your pruning hooks into spears; Let the weak say, "I am strong."

—Joel 3:10, nkjv

For assuredly, I say to you, whoever says to this mountain, "Be removed and be cast into the sea," and does not doubt in his heart, but believes that those things he says will be done, he will have whatever he says. Therefore I say to you, whatever things you ask when you pray, believe that you receive them, and you will have them.

—MARK 11:23–24, NKJV

For the eyes of the LORD are on the righteous, And His ears are open to their prayers; But the face of the LORD is against those who do evil.

—1 PETER 3:12, NKJV

Again I say to you that if two of you agree on earth concerning anything that they ask, it will be done for them by My Father in heaven.

—MATTHEW 18:19, NKJV

For where two or three are gathered together in My name, I am there in the midst of them.

—MATTHEW 18:20, NKJV

But without faith it is impossible to please Him, for he who comes to God must believe that He is, and that He is a rewarder of those who diligently seek Him.

—HEBREWS 11:6, NKJV

But He was wounded for our transgressions, He was bruised for our iniquities; The chastisement for our peace was upon Him, And by His stripes we *are healed*.

—ISAIAH 53:5, NKJV, EMPHASIS ADDED

Now faith is the substance of things hoped for, the evidence of things not seen.

—HEBREWS 11:1, NKJV

So then faith comes by hearing, and hearing by the word of God.

—ROMANS 10:17, NKJV

Draw near to God and He will draw near to you. Cleanse your hands, you sinners; and purify your hearts, you double-minded.

—JAMES 4:8, NKJV

If My people who are called by My name will humble themselves, and pray and seek My face, and turn from their wicked ways, then I will hear from heaven, and will forgive their sin and heal their land.

—2 CHRONICLES 7:14, NKJV

Blessed is the man who endures temptation; for when he has been approved, he will receive the crown of life which the Lord has promised to those who love Him.

—JAMES 1:12, NKJV

Now we know that God does not hear sinners; but if anyone is a worshiper of God and does His will, He hears him.

—JOHN 9:31, NKJV

For if our heart condemns us, God is greater than our heart, and knows all things. Beloved, if our heart does not condemn us, we have confidence toward God. And whatever we ask we receive from Him, because we keep His commandments and do those things that are pleasing in His sight.

—1 JOHN 3:20–22, NKJV

Now this is the confidence that we have in Him, that if we ask anything according to His will, He hears us. And if we know that He hears us, whatever we ask, we know that we have the petitions that we have asked of Him.

—1 JOHN 5:14–15, NKJV

God's Promises to Pray for Peace

Peace I leave with you, My peace I give to you; not as the world gives do I give to you. Let not your heart be troubled, neither let it be afraid. You have heard Me say to you, "I am going away and coming back to you." If you loved Me, you would rejoice because I said, "I am going to the Father," for My Father is greater than I.

—John 14:27–28, nkjv

You will keep him in perfect peace, Whose mind is stayed on You, because he trusts in You.

—Isaiah 26:3, nkjv

I will both lie down in peace, and sleep; For you alone, O Lord, make me dwell in safety.

—Psalm 4:8, nkjv

These things I have spoken to you, that in Me you may have peace. In the world you will have tribulation; but be of good cheer, I have overcome the world.

—John 16:33, nkjv

Be anxious for nothing, but in everything by prayer and supplication, with thanksgiving, let your requests be made known to God; and the peace of God, which surpasses all understanding, will guard your hearts and minds through Christ Jesus.

—Philippians 4:6–7, nkjv

The Lord is my shepherd; I shall not want. He makes me lie down in green pastures; He leads me beside the still waters. He restores my soul; He leads me in the paths of righteousness For His name's sake.

—Psalm 23:1–3, nkjv

And we know that all things work together for good to those who love God, to those who are called according to His purpose.

—ROMANS 8:28, NKJV

Therefore submit to God. Resist the devil and he will flee from you.

—JAMES 4:7, NKJV

Behold, I will bring it health and healing; I will heal them and reveal to them the abundance of peace and truth.

—JEREMIAH 33:6, NKJV

Chapter 7

KEY SEVEN: THINGS YOU SHOULD ALWAYS REMEMBER

A lways be alert of Satan's activities, his deadly traps and schemes of disaster, because he is always plotting ways to trap us. Second Corinthians 2:10–11 tells us, "But one whom you forgive anything, I forgive also; for indeed what I have forgiven, if I have forgiven anything, I did it for your sakes in the presence of Christ, so that no advantage would be taken of us by Satan, for we are not ignorant of his schemes." His sole purpose is to take captive and destroy God's people, Christians and unbelievers as well.

> The thief does not come except to steal, and to kill, and to destroy. I have come that they may have life, and that they may have it more abundantly. I am the good shepherd. The good shepherd gives His life for the sheep.
> —JOHN 10:10–11, NKJV

The enemy is happier when he knows he can entice us to do his will, which is to destroy us, our minds, marriages, bodies, and our souls. Jesus saved us from Satan's power. We are redeemed by the body and blood of Jesus Christ. Whatever Satan has planned for us will not stand because we are all children of God, and God does not allow anything to happen to His beloved children when we are walking in obedience to Christ.

We recognize Satan's attempts in our lives by the power of the Holy Spirit. You can rebuke these endeavors in the name of Jesus Christ and they will turn out as blessings to you. The opposite of what Satan intends will occur; they will be blessings in honor of God. When you become aware of Satan's attempts in your life and turn from them, then God turns what was meant to harm you into a blessing.

> No weapon formed against you will prosper; And every tongue that accuses you in judgment you will condemn. This is the heritage of the servants of the LORD, And their vindication is from Me, declares the LORD.
>
> —ISAIAH 54:17

Satan does not have any authority over the life of a believer. He is a liar, and a thief. Second Corinthians 11:14 says, "No wonder, for even Satan disguises himself as an angel of light." His sole purpose is to kill or destroy God's people, but only if we allow him to. We have to stand firm on God's words. We have to constantly seek God's words and presence. Satan will flee from your holy presence when you began to praise God. Holy Spirit power has a devastating effect on the enemy.

Remember that God loves you and would never forsake you. Joshua 1:5 says, "No man will be able to stand before you all the days of your life. Just as I have been with Moses, I will be with you; I will not fail you or forsake you." You are a precious, rare jewel, and precious jewels are treasured. God is the only key you will ever need throughout your lifetime. He is the key to love, devotion, and peace of heart. He is our great Protector and Provider.

Not having God in your life is like living in an unlocked house. And in today's time, that is unsafe; we are asking or inviting trouble into our homes. We need the Key of protection not only for ourselves, but for our children and for future generations.

Never take current situations for granted. What you see now is not promised tomorrow. Plant a good seed now and expect a good harvest in the time to come; but plant a bad and ungodly seed now, and you will harvest a disaster. Remember that the children of today are our future; we cannot forsake our future. Our children and grandchildren will reap the benefits, whether good or bad. "Do not be deceived, God is not mocked; for whatever a man sows, this he will also reap" (Gal. 6:7). God has a plan for each of our lives; all we have to do is allow His plan to be fulfilled by first surrendering our lives to Him, Jesus Christ. When you do, things will change in your life: blessings will come and you will have peace in your life that many will not understand, but they will envy you because of it.

So stand firm on God's Word and on solid ground which is Jesus Christ. Tell Satan this is your house and he doesn't have authority here anymore—*not ever*—in the name of Jesus Christ. Luke 10:19 tells us, "Behold, I have given you authority to tread on serpents and scorpions, and over all the power of the enemy, and nothing will injure you." Remember, Satan cannot harm you when you use the power within yourself, which is the Holy Spirit. Call on Jesus when the enemy attacks your mind with lies. Stay guarded by being prayerful and armed in the presence of God.

All born-again believers have the authority to bind any illness, poverty, or lack in the name of Jesus Christ and loose healing, prosperity, and freedom from all generational addictions, diseases, and disorders over their family in the name of Jesus Christ. "I will give you the keys of the kingdom of heaven; and whatever you bind on earth shall have been bound in heaven, and whatever you loose on earth shall have been loosed in heaven" (Matt. 16:19). God's children deserve happiness and not despair; joy and not loneliness; peace and not worry; a sound mind and not one of confusion. All these things Satan has tried to steal but, by God's power, Satan is defeated. His attacks can and will not stand. When you stand with God, your enemies will be your footstool; they will only elevate you.

> Therefore, since the children share in flesh and blood, He Himself likewise also partook of the same, that through death He might render powerless him who had the power of death, this is, the devil, and might free those who through fear of death were subject to slavery all their lives.
> —HEBREWS 2:14–15

Remember God is your light. He is determined to bring you out of darkness, so let your light shine by imitating Christ wherever you go, whatever you do, and to whomever you may meet. Ephesians 5:1–2 tells us, "Therefore be imitators of God, as beloved children; and walk in love, just as Christ also loved you and gave Himself up for us, an offering and a sacrifice to God as a fragrant aroma." They will know you are a child of the Most High God, a child blessed by the power of the Holy Spirit, because your actions will display the fruit of the Spirit:

> But the fruit of the Spirit is love, joy, peace, patience, kindness, goodness, faithfulness, gentleness, self-control.
> —GALATIANS 5:22–23

Chapter 8

KEY EIGHT: WORDS OF WISDOM

Have you ever depended on someone for a favor, advice, or leadership? Maybe it was your mother, sister, brother, or a close friend that you counted on for something and they failed to come through for you. Do you know that Jesus is always there at your side waiting for you to ask, knock, or mention His name? Jesus is your mother, father, sister, and also your brother all in one. He is everything you will ever need. He is the light that guides each one of us when we call on Him for help. Some of us acknowledge Jesus only when we are at our breaking point or when we have exhausted every other route of hope before trusting Him. When everyone we thought we could count on failed to come through for us, there is Jesus the whole time waving His hands in front of us saying, "(Your name), here I am; why don't you trust me with this situation or concern?"

Some burdens are not meant for us to carry. When we try to handle life's problems in our own strength, it is like trying to pick up a two-ton brick by hand; we just cannot do it. We have to give Jesus our burdens and problems that overwhelm us by saying, "Lord, take this from me; I give it to you; it's too much for me, amen." Then pick yourself up and keep going. Your problem is resolved, it is no more. Your may not see it in the natural, but God is at work on your behalf to bring that problem or concern to pass. Until you see changes, remind yourself daily that God is working on the situation. Believe and you will receive!

According to the Psalms, Jesus bears our burdens daily: "Blessed be the Lord, who *daily* bears our burden, The God who is our salvation. Selah" (Ps. 68:19, emphasis added). Walk away and do not look back. Your faith will set you free; you have put the problem into God's hands. According to 2 Corinthians 5:7, "We walk by faith, not by sight." Everything is possible with God. Luke 18:27 says, "But He said, 'The things that are impossible with people are possible with God.'" Matthew tells us to ask and we will receive: "And all things you ask in prayer, believing, you will receive" (Matt. 21:22). Knock and the door will be opened. Ask for a leader and you shall be led. For today is not promised to us, our time is short; the future is now. Call on Jesus to help you and lead your life.

Money cannot solve our problems; it can only buy time or delay circumstances. Jesus is the problem solver, the circumstance remover. He is the present and the future. He is everything we need. Why don't you give Him a try?

Many of us have problems in our lives that cause us to worry, thus causing physical illnesses. It may end up as a psychological problem or may cause a heart attack, stroke, hypertension, or even heart palpitations due to constant worrying. Whatever these burdens may cause, Jesus tells us that we do not have to go through this. We are not alone. He is always waiting to help you. Call on Him and He will come; He will reveal Himself to you. Jesus wants to help you with all your concerns: loneliness; financial problems; overspending; debt; addictions such as smoking, alcoholism, pornography; homosexuality or any other sexual problems, etc. There is nothing that Jesus cannot help you with. There is much power in the name of Jesus. Call on Him!

Chapter 9

KEY NINE: WORDS OF ENCOURAGEMENT

We should build one another up with words of encourage-ment, but we should always seek God to encourage us daily. Reading the Bible helps you understand the ways of God and it also helps you grow spiritually. Daily meditation in the Word of God helps us to stay in tune with the Father. Always seek God's presence by worshiping and praising Him. Find a quiet place and develop a relationship with God. Do not be afraid to empty out your heart before the Lord. Tell God what or how you feel, and expect Him to answer your prayer in whatever way and time He chooses; we serve a patient God. He is never in a hurry, and His timing is always right, exactly when we need Him. Never think that your question is petty or not important, because everything we do is important to God. He is pleased when we seek Him out or ask Him about issues in our lives. When God encourages you, you are to encourage others. We are to be a blessing to one another. Become a witness of Christ's goodness and how He has changed you and blessed you. God will use you to save others and help them in their Christian walk.

Lift each other up in prayer, as the Father lifts us up when we pray to Him. Never think that you have to go to a particular place to pray to God. God is with you always. Try talking to Him while you are driving, cooking, or relaxing. When you awake ask Him to lead your day for His purpose. Begin your day by putting on the armor of God. When you retire for the evening, thank

Him for blessing your day and ask Him to wake you up in the morning. Make it a habit to talk to God. He is always waiting to hear from you. Second Chronicles 7:14 tells us, "[If] My people who are called by My name humble themselves and pray and seek My face and turn from their wicked ways, then I will hear from heaven, will forgive their sin and will heal their land." Tell Him your concerns or problems and ask for His help. God knows that life is hard, especially when we are out of His will.

We need God's daily encouragement for a successful life. Look at the flowers and how they grow, look at the birds in the sky; if God feeds plants and birds, He surely will nourish our souls and bodies for growth and peace. "Look at the birds of the air, that they do not sow, nor reap nor gather into barns, and yet your heavenly Father feeds them. Are you not worth much more than they?" (Matt. 6:26). Never think of yourself as unimportant to God, or that you do not deserve an answer from God. The "creature" Satan implants those thoughts in your mind, and when he does, you are to rebuke him in the holy name of Jesus Christ and he will flee from you. Satan has to flee from your presence because He hates the name of Jesus Christ.

You are hated by the creature, Satan, because you believe in the name of Jesus Christ and there is much power in His name. His name represents His blood that was shed for us on Calvary. When you are washed in His blood by receiving and believing in Him, no evil shall come against you when you use His name in times of need.

> The name of the LORD is a strong tower; The righteous run
> to it and are safe.
>
> —PROVERBS 18:10, NKJV

Psalm 23:1 says, "The LORD is my shepherd; I shall not want." God does not want you to want for anything; in other words, do not worry about tomorrow, or next year, or twenty thousand years from now. Do not worry what to eat, drink, or wear. Keep your eyes fixed on the Savior and He will provide you with what you need.

Many people have weight problems—or think they have a weight problem; but in God's eyes you are perfect when your spirit is aligned with His. When the time comes to meet the Lord, the body will not matter. God is concerned with the soul. So get the spirit aligned with the Father first, then, with the help of the Holy Spirit working within you, God will show you how to overcome addictions. Pray and fast for Him to help you change your diet. God does desire us to be healthy.

Allow the Holy Spirit to guide you in ending the strongholds in your life that are displeasing to God. If it is food, alcohol, drugs, or any other addiction, it is now a "*has been*"; because when you receive Jesus and allow His Spirit to lead your life, the Spirit will show you how to defeat the problem. He will strengthen you to overcome the desires of the flesh. Anything is possible with Jesus: "And Jesus said to him, 'If you can?' All things are possible to him who believes" (Mark 9:23). The Holy Spirit will help you to resist these temptations. The Spirit will rule your body, mind, and soul. All you have to do is allow it to take control. Allow it to rule over your flesh. Learn to say no to your flesh and your flesh will obey. Stay away from the places, people, and things that will tempt you into doing old habits that you know God is calling you out of.

Remember your body is the temple of God, it stores the Holy Spirit. We have to keep our bodies holy in every way.

Chapter 10

KEY TEN: THINGS TO DO

W hen you kneel to pray, allow the Holy Spirit to guide you on what and for whom to pray; the Holy Spirit is our leader. The Father and the Holy Spirit know what you need to pray for; the Holy Spirit reveals it to you. Pray with your mind guided by the Holy Spirit, and if you have the gift of tongues (the Holy Spirit prays to God for you in a heavenly language), allow the Holy Spirit to pray to God for you. It is especially important to pray in the Holy Spirit because the Holy Spirit intercedes to God on your behalf. The Holy Spirit prays the perfect will of God (for you).

The apostle Paul wrote about praying in tongues:

> For anyone who speaks in a tongue does not speak to people but to God. Indeed, no one understands them; they utter mysteries by the Spirit.
> —1 CORINTHIANS 14:2, NIV

> For if I pray in a tongue, my spirit prays, but my mind is unfruitful. So what shall I do? I will pray with my spirit, but I will also pray with my understanding; I will sing with my spirit, but I will also sing with my understanding.
> —1 CORINTHIANS 14:14–15, NIV

The Bible says that when the Holy Spirit descended in Cornelius' house, the whole house began to speak in tongues. Cornelius was seeking God, and God revealed Himself to Cornelius. God will reveal Himself when you seek Him as well.

> While Peter was still speaking these words, the Holy Spirit fell upon all those who heard the word. And those of the circumcision who believed were astonished, as many as came with Peter, because the gift of the Holy Spirit had been poured out on the Gentiles also. For they heard them speak with tongues and magnify God.
>
> —ACTS 10:44–46, NKJV

> In the same way, the Spirit helps us in our weakness. We do not know what we ought to pray for, but the Spirit himself intercedes for us through wordless groans. And he who searches our hearts knows the mind of the Spirit, because the Spirit intercedes for God's people in accordance with the will of God.
>
> —ROMANS 8:26–27, NIV

If you do not have your heavenly language yet, ask God to give it to you. God's Word says, we do not have because we do not ask, and God is a rewarder of those who seek Him.

> You lust and do not have; so you commit murder. You are envious and cannot obtain; so you fight and quarrel. *You do not have because you do not ask.*
>
> —JAMES 4:2, EMPHASIS ADDED

> But without faith it is impossible to please Him, for he who comes to God must believe that He is, and that He is a rewarder of those who *diligently seek Him.*
>
> —HEBREWS 11:6, NKJV, EMPHASIS ADDED

About three years after I became saved, my husband led my mother to give her life to Christ. Then years later when my mother was visiting me I heard her praying in tongues. She told me that she received her heavenly prayer language when she stepped off of a city bus. I expressed to God that I wanted my heavenly prayer language as well. So, I began to seek God for it in prayer.

Approximately six months to one year later, I was praying in the bathroom concerning something heavy on my heart. Then all of a sudden, I felt the presence of the Holy Spirit and out of my mouth came my heavenly prayer language that the apostle Paul talked about. I was praying in tongues. Now I pray in tongues and with my mind every day. It is wonderful to have the Holy Spirit pray for you. The Holy Spirit is truly our helper. Thanks to Jesus! You can have the same experience if you do not pray in tongues already. If God gave it to me, He will give it to you as well. The Bible tells us He does not show favoritism (Acts 10:34).

Pray daily, especially when you awake in the morning. Remember to put on the armor of God before starting your day. The armor of God will help you to walk in the spirit and not the flesh. The more you pray, the more your prayers will be answered. Encourage others to pray as well. Be encouraged to pray for the needs of others, especially the lost and Israel. God commands us to pray for Israel:

> Pray for the peace of Jerusalem: "May they prosper who love you."
>
> —PSALM 122:6

When you pray, always give glory to God first; give Him praise and honor for He is an honorable God, then ask God your prayer request. Worshiping God brings you into His presence. He knows what you will ask. God knows everything. Never pray for something out of envy or strife, for those prayers will go unanswered. Always pray for blessings for others: the sick, lonely, depressed, and for those who do not know God; your prayers will be heard. Empty your heart of any sin and repent of anything you have done that was against the Word of God before coming before the Lord in prayer.

> Therefore, confess your sins to one another, and pray for one another so that you may be healed. The effective prayer of a righteous man can accomplish much.
>
> —JAMES 5:16

Forgive anyone that may have caused you harm in any way before coming into God's presence, because His presence is holy and God is intolerable of sin. Matthew 6:14–15 says, "For if you forgive others for their transgressions, your heavenly Father will also forgive you. But if you do not forgive others, then your Father will not forgive your transgressions." Trust God with your concerns.

Try fasting sometimes when in prayer because fasting glorifies God and it also cleanses your body of anything unholy. Remember, God is concerned with every aspect of your life. He welcomes you into His presence. Repent of any sin before coming into God's presence in prayer.

> I cried to Him with my mouth, And He was extolled with my tongue. If I regard wickedness in my heart, The Lord will not hear; But certainly God has heard; He has given heed to the voice of my prayer.
>
> —PSALM 66:17–19

> Behold, the LORD's hand is not so short That it cannot save; Nor is His ear so dull That it cannot hear. But your iniquities have made a separation between you and your God, And your sins have hidden His face from you so that He does not hear.
>
> —ISAIAH 59:1–2

Pray for your enemies because God will bless you as you bless them and He will cause peace between them and you:

> But I say to you, love your enemies and pray for those who persecute you.
>
> —MATTHEW 5:44

> When a man's ways please the LORD, He makes even his enemies to be at peace with him.
>
> —PROVERBS 16:7, NKJV

Chapter 11

KEY ELEVEN: WHY THINGS HAPPEN TO US

Unfavorable things happen in our lives for many different reasons. One reason is because we are not following the commands of the Lord. Other reasons may be because we are not spending time in God's presence or we don't allow the Holy Spirit to lead our lives. If we were led by Him, these things would not occur. When we surrender our mind, body, and soul to the Lord, He prevents the unfavorable from crossing our paths. Many things happen to us because of disobedience to God.

Have you ever had a thought to do something for someone or to go somewhere and you just put that thought on the back burner and never did it? God puts ideas and thoughts on our minds to encourage us to do the right thing. When we fail to listen to Him, we open the door for things to take place in our lives. We walk away from His hand of protection. We walk away from His guidance. In other words, we tell God that we will do what we want to. We are our own bosses. Meditating on God's Word and spending time with God in prayer will keep you in His will.

Many of us need to allow God to take control of our lives. The way you do that is by telling God that you are a sinner and asking Him to forgive you of all sin: present, past, and future. Humble yourself in His presence and glorify and praise His name. Then ask Him to take complete control of your life, of all situations or burdens that are on your heart. Then, thank Him for doing so. When you walk away from His presence, leave all these things with Him. Leave them on the floor; do not think about your problems, think about the problem solver, God. Isaiah 26:3 tells us, "The steadfast of mind You will keep in perfect peace, Because he trusts in You." It does not matter what the problem is, trust and pray knowing that God is in control.

Sometimes things happen to us to test our actions: will it be a godly or ungodly reaction? It is not the situation that is important, but how you respond to the situation is what the Lord is looking for. Remember God is in control of everything that happens. It is Satan that brings havoc in our lives because we open the door called sin. Remember to follow the Holy Spirit in your decision-making.

Another reason may be because we are doing the will of the Lord and the enemy, Satan, sends something or someone to distract us or cause us to stumble or even get out of the will of God. Remember Job and his sufferings and how he responded to God while he waited for God to heal him? Job was faithful to God even through his suffering, and then God rewarded him. Ask God to give you a discerning spirit in these situations. God will help you to discern. God can bring you out of any situation. Trust Him! Obey the commands of the Lord and everything will fall into place.

> And we know God causes all things to work together for good to those who love God, to those who are called according to His purpose
>
> —ROMANS 8:28

Chapter 12

KEY TWELVE: WHY GOD HATES DOUBT

W hat is doubt? According to Webster's dictionary, doubt means uncertainty of belief or opinion that often inter- feres with decision-making, an inclination not to believe or accept. Doubt is disbelief or questioning whether something will take place, not being confident in the results or actions taken place. Doubt or disbelief has no room in the kingdom of God.

> Truly I say to you, whoever says to this mountain, "Be taken up and cast into the sea," and does not doubt in his heart, but believes that what he says is going to happen, it will be granted him. Therefore I say to you, all things for which you pray and ask, believe that you have received them, and they will be granted to you.
>
> —MARK 11:23–24

God's words are true and everlasting. To doubt God or His words is to doubt the very existence of God and His power. If we could grab a hold of the true meaning of doubt in God or His abilities, we as Christians could not continue to walk in disbelief of His power, because to do so would degrade His power (which is supernatural) or undermine His existence.

We know what the Bible says about God; He is all knowing, all powerful, the Creator of heaven and earth and everything on the earth and in heaven. To doubt God is to doubt what the Bible says about Him and doubt the supernatural wonders of our lives.

God created every human on the face of the earth. Matthew 10:30–31 tells us, "The very hairs of your head are all numbered. So do not fear; you are more valuable than many sparrows." This verse says He knows every strand of hair on our heads. A God who is concerned with every inch of us from the inside out should be trusted to heal us physically and emotionally. A God who cares about the number of hair strands on our head must care about the others parts as well. God knows when disease or disorders strike against us by the evil one, Satan. Christ tells us in His Word that He has overcome the world; Satan's power over our lives has been broken.

> These things I have spoken to you, so that in Me you may have peace. In the world you have tribulation, but take courage; I have overcome the world.
>
> —JOHN 16:33

> The one who practices sin is of the devil; for the devil has sinned from the beginning. The Son of God appeared for this purpose, to destroy the works of the devil [by shedding His blood].
>
> —1 JOHN 3:8

When you take a stand and declare that Jesus' blood has more power than the enemy will ever have and begin to speak words of healing over your sickness, you will be healed. When you plead the blood of Jesus over yourself and your loved ones, Satan's hold or attack has to vanish because the Word of God says in 1 John 4:4, "You are from God, little children, and have overcome them; *because greater is He who is in you than he who is in the world*" (emphasis added). Stand and believe on God's Word and it will deliver you at all times.

God knew of sickness and disease before the fall of man (Adam). He has placed a perfect plan into being to rid the world of plagues and disease, by believing in the power of the blood of Jesus Christ. The second Adam (Jesus) came to repair what was broken by the first Adam when he bowed down to Satan in the Garden of Eden.

Unfortunately, many people remain in a state of sickness because of disbelief. They do not take God's Word or His power seriously. The Bible says in Matthew 13:58, "And He did not do many miracles there because of their unbelief."

When you believe in the power of God by evidence of His creation and by developing a personal relationship with Jesus, which He offers to all who are willing to receive and believe in Him, then there is nothing that will be able to harm or overtake you. When you began to speak healing to your body (disease or disorder) in the name of Jesus Christ by the power of the Holy Spirit, the disease has to leave because Jesus has already paid for your healing on the cross. All you must do is see yourself healed (take hold of the vision).

You may ask, How can I have a personal relationship with God? The Bible says in James 4:2, "You lust and do not have; so you commit murder. You are envious and cannot obtain; so you fight and quarrel. *You do not have because you do not ask*" (emphasis added). Do what Romans 10:9 tells us to do, which is to ask Jesus into your life and believe that He is the Lord and that He died for your sins. Ask Him into your heart and to help you develop a personal relationship with Him. Ask Him to fill you with His precious Holy Spirit. Spend time daily with God and meditate on His Word. The more you spend time with God, the more you will experience His presence.

Use the Scriptures to ward off the enemy when he attacks you; whether it is through your thoughts, emotions, or physically.

Use the Word of God towards Satan and he will flee from your presence. The Bible tells us to resist the devil and he will flee (James 4:7). Do not use your own words when rebuking the tempter, but use the Word of God, just as Jesus did when He was tempted in the desert by Satan:

> Then Jesus said to him, "Go, Satan! For it is written, 'YOU SHALL WORSHIP THE LORD YOUR GOD, AND SERVE HIM ONLY.'" Then the devil left Him; and behold, angels came and began to minister to Him.
> —MATTHEW 4:10–11

I believe without a doubt that when we use the Scriptures in the name of Jesus over our situations, God sends His angels to minister to us as well (to help us). When Satan says you are sick or not healed, quote Isaiah 53:5, "He was wounded for our transgressions, He was bruised for our iniquities; The chastisement for our peace was upon Him, *And by His stripes we are healed [I am healed!]*" (NKJV, emphasis added).

God has also given us the power to bind and loose things over ourselves and others. "I will give you the keys of the kingdom of heaven; and whatever you bind on earth shall have been bound in heaven, and whatever you loose on earth shall have been loosed in heaven" (Matt. 16:19). If you are sick you can pray this as well: "I bind the spirit of infirmity from me and I loose total healing over my body in the name of Jesus."

Remember to repent of any sin when asking God to heal you. God wants us to be striving to walk upright before Him, so He can honor our prayers. We are not perfect by any means; that's why God had to send His Son. We have the Cross to go to when we sin. We have to be quick and ask God to forgive us in the name of Jesus. Jesus' blood covers *all* sin; it is not an excuse to sin.

Nothing is too hard for God to do: heal sicknesses, strengthen marriages, mend relationships, change wayward children, solve problems and concerns, or heal finances. Ask God in the name of Jesus and believe while you wait and expect positive results. All things are possible with God to them that believe (Mark 9:23).

When you read God's Word and meditated on it, pay attention to God's character and the teachings of Christ. The Bible teaches us how to live and trust in God for all things. Look to the Creator and not the creature. Worship the problem solver and not the problem. If you spend more time talking about the problem than you do in prayer and worship of God, then you are elevating the problem. Trust in Him and not in them.

> And we know that God causes all things to work together for good to those who love God, to those who are called according to His purpose.
> —ROMANS 8:28

Your words are powerful. If you speak good things into your life, good things will happen; if you speak negative things into your life, negative things will happen. What you speak you will receive. Proverbs 18:21 says, "Death and life are in the power of the tongue, And those who love it will eat its fruit." God showed me the meaning of this scripture and how we speak negative words over ourselves without knowing the consequences of those words. About five years ago, I came home from work and I had this aching abdominal pain. The pain was on the right side of my abdomen and it was painful and tender to touch. It started off as a mild ache, then it became excruciating. Being a nurse, I told my husband that I thought I had appendicitis. The pain became worse during the night and it was difficult for me to sleep.

The only thing I could think about was to pray. So, I went into the bathroom and I got on my knees and called out to God in prayer. I prayed out loud saying, *God, your Word says in Isaiah 53:5 that I am healed; by Jesus' stripes, I am healed. I receive my healing in Jesus' name, please take this pain away. I bind the pain and loose total healing over myself right now, in Jesus' name.* I was crying out to God because I was in pain. Then I went back to bed, trying not to awaken Jerry. I had told him earlier that I might need to go to the emergency room.

As I lay in bed, I heard these words spoken to me, like someone was standing right next to my bed. To this day I believe it was the voice of an angel. The Spirit of the Lord said, "If you would not speak it upon yourself you would not have it." I suddenly opened my eyes in amazement and just lay still, thinking, where did those words come from? I realized it was God, went back to the bathroom, got on my knees again, and repented for speaking an illness over myself. I asked God to forgive me for saying that I have appendicitis.

I was claiming the illness instead of speaking healing over my body by claiming the promise of Isaiah 53:5, "He was wounded for our transgressions, He was bruised for our iniquities; The chastisement for our peace was upon Him, And by His stripes, we are healed." I was speaking death and not life. What we speak we will have, because God says that death and life are in the power of the tongue. Our words have power! After praying I went back to bed; the pain left and I have never had it again. Jesus healed me that night. Praise His name!

God was teaching me the power that our words have and about His power to heal me. Our words can bring life or death into our lives. He also taught me that His Word is true, alive, and powerful when we believe what it says. The Bible has many of God's promises that He wants us to take seriously, the good promises as well as the bad promises. God gave us promises if we obey and trust Him and promises if we do not obey Him. An example is given in

Deuteronomy chapter 28. God tells us the blessings that will overtake us if we are obedient and it also tells us of the curses that will happen if we are disobedient. They are promises that God gave to the children of Israel and they still apply to us today.

We have to read God's Word and learn of as many promises as we can. We have to claim them for ourselves and our families because they are true and bring life to every believer. God's Word teaches us that God's people perish because of lack of knowledge (Hosea 4:6, "My people are destroyed for lack of knowledge," NKJV). When I had the abdominal pain, I did not know that I was speaking an illness on myself, until God made it known to me. He reminded me what His Word says in Proverbs 18:21. That's when I realized that I had to learn more about what God's Word said, so I could use it to bless me and my family. I pray God's Scriptures daily as promises for me and my family and I claim them, all those that I want to see come to pass in our lives.

Another time God healed me was when I had an earache. If you have ever had one, it can be quite painful. It was an intermittent type of pain. While I was lying in bed praying to God for healing; I quoted Isaiah 53:5, then I bound the pain and loosed total healing over my ear. I fell asleep, and then I felt the presence of the Lord (it was like a strong wind over me). I knew God was letting me know that He had heard my prayer and was healing me. I have never had an earache since. Thank you, Jesus, because of the Cross, we are healed.

I do believe that God heals through doctors as well. But never speak an illness over yourself. I am not saying to deny the illness, just don't give it any authority over you. You have authority and power over it with your words. That's what God is telling us.

The Bible says that "faith comes by hearing, and hearing by the Word of God" (Rom. 10:17, NKJV). When my abdomen was hurting me, I did not deny that something was wrong. God just didn't want me to speak appendicitis over myself. When I was in the bathroom praying and reminding God what His Word said about being healed through Jesus' stripes (like He forgot), I now realize that my faith was in action. My faith came from reading and hearing His Word being preached. I was quoting His Scripture back to Him out loud. I took His Word seriously that I was healed. God wanted me to speak healing over myself and not sickness. God will not override your will. He gives us a free will. He does not force anyone to do anything. But He does discipline us (Heb. 12:5).

Now I never speak any illness over myself. Do not say, "I think I am getting sick," or, "I think I am catching a cold." I used to say things like that until God showed me otherwise. We should speak only health, healing, and blessings over ourselves. That's what God wants. We are His children and He wants the very best for us. I believe when we speak negative things over ourselves and loved ones we open the door for the enemy to come in and make them happen.

The Bible tells us in John 10:10, "The thief comes only to steal and kill and destroy; I came that they may have life, and have it abundantly." The enemy will tell you things like, "You are not healed," "Your marriage will never get any better," "Your child will never come to God," "You will never conceive a child," or, "You will never get out of debt." Whatever you are believing God for, Satan will tell you the opposite; and we all know that the Bible says he is a liar, so when he tells you that, the opposite must be true. If we do not know what the Word of God says, the enemy can steal all of our blessings right from under our noses. I thank God for His Word and the promises that it contains for us.

Another time God healed me was when I hit my toe on something. When I tried to put pressure on that toe to walk, it was painful. I would put my hand on my toe and say Isaiah 53:5, and pray for Jesus to heal me. I would bind the pain and loose healing over my toe, in the name of Jesus Christ. After almost a week my toe was still hurting. One morning I awoke and remembered a dream I had that night. I dreamed that I ran into the kitchen telling my mother that God had healed my toe. After recalling the dream, I got out of bed and when I put pressure on that toe, the pain was gone and it never came back, thanks to Jesus.

Think positive thoughts and speak victory over your life by casting out any negative thoughts of doubt, and continue to believe what God has told you and what the Bible promises. By being obedient to God and believing what He says will happen, you will receive the promise.

> From the days of John the Baptist until now the kingdom of heaven suffers violence, and violent men take it by force.
> —MATTHEW 11:12

Matthew is telling us that the kingdom of heaven, which is the promises of God, has to be taken by force. Be persistent with your prayers. Just as Jesus teaches in Luke 18:1–8:

> Now He was telling them a parable to show that at all times they ought to pray and not lose heart, saying, "In a certain city there was a judge who did not fear God and did not respect man. There was a widow in that city, and she kept coming to him, saying, 'Give me legal protection from my opponent.' For a while he was unwilling; but afterward he said to himself, 'Even thought I do not fear God nor respect man, yet because this widow bothers me, I will give her legal protection, otherwise by continually coming she will wear me out.'" And the Lord said, "Hear what the unrighteous judge said; now, will not God bring about justice for His elect who cry to Him day and night, and will He delay long over them? I tell you that He will bring about justice for them quickly. However, when the Son of Man comes, will He find faith on the earth?"

You have the Holy Spirit inside of you; God says that the Holy Spirit is our helper. Remember the power that God has given you to bind and loose. If you are having problems in your marriage, for example, when you pray for your marriage, say: "I bind the spirit of strife from my marriage and I loose love and peace and restoration in my marriage in the name of Jesus." If you have a child that is rebelling, you can pray this: "God says whatever I bind on earth, He will bind in heaven and whatever I loose on earth He will loose in heaven, so I bind the spirit of rebellion from Susie and I loose peace, love, joy, and a heart obedient to God and those in authority over her right now in the name of Jesus." Another example would be for your finances: quote Matthew 16:19, then say, "I bind poverty and lack in my finances and I loose prosperity and God's abundance in my home in the name of Jesus."

You can also find scriptures where God promises to bless those who walk upright before Him, such as Philippians 4:19, "And my God shall apply all my needs according to His riches in glory by Christ Jesus" (NKJV). Expect God to open up opportunities for increase in your life and to move in your health, marriage, finances, relationships, and your children. We as believers have to be girded up daily in our armor of God because Satan and his demons will do all that they possibly can to try to prove to God that we are not steadfast. Isaiah 26:3 says, "You will keep in perfect peace those whose minds are steadfast, because they trust in you" (NIV). Pray your promise scriptures daily before you start your day; you will have armored yourself in what God says, so if the enemy tries to discourage you during your day, you are already armed with God's Word in you to use against his attacks. You will be victorious! Make the choice to believe God, no matter how it looks.

Chapter 13

KEY THIRTEEN: THE UNLIMITED POWER OF GOD

Have you ever wondered why it takes some men a lifetime to accomplish great things, but when the power of God is with him it can only take an hour to accomplish that same thing? There is a big difference in relying on your own strength and relying on the power of God to accomplish something in your life. You may say, yeah, but it takes a lot of faith to rely on and trust in God in doing great things. No, the Bible tells us that it only takes a mustard seed-sized faith to move God to act on your behalf. Matthew, 17:20 says (NASB), "And He said to them, 'Because of the littleness of your faith; for truly I say to you, if you have faith the size of a mustard seed, you will say to this mountain, "Move from here to there," and it will move; and nothing will be impossible to you.'"

When you take your limits off of God, then God can do more things in your life. The level of belief determines the provision of God. In other words, what you believe God for is what you will receive. Keep your vision big and focus on seeing it come to pass.

Have you wondered how some people accomplish many things in their lifespan more than others? God rewards your obedience and trust in Him.

When Abraham obeyed and trusted God, God blessed him. The Lord told Abraham to sacrifice his only son, Isaac, to God. Abraham believed that God would provide a sacrifice.

> Isaac spoke to Abraham his father and said, "My father!" And he said, "Here I am, my son." And he said, "Behold, the fire and the wood, but where is the lamb for the burnt offering?" Abraham said, "God will provide for Himself the lamb for the burnt offering, my son." So the two of them walked on together.
>
> —GENESIS 22:7–8

The Lord did not want the sacrifice, but only to reveal Abraham's obedience and trust in God.

> But Samuel replied: "Does the LORD delight in burnt offerings and sacrifices as much as in obeying the voice of the LORD? To obey is better than sacrifice, and to heed is better than the fat of rams."
>
> —1 SAMUEL 15:22, NIV

> Then the angel of the LORD called to Abraham a second time from heaven, and said, "By Myself I have sworn, declares the LORD, because you have done this thing and have not withheld your son, your only son, indeed I will greatly bless you, and I will greatly multiply your seed as the stars of the heavens and as the sand which is on the seashore; and your seed shall possess the gate of their enemies. In your seed all the nations of the earth shall be blessed, because you have obeyed My voice."
>
> —GENESIS 22:15–18

If you trust God with bringing only little things to pass, then that's what you'll get. God wants to bring the big things to pass in your life as well. You have to trust and believe Him to do it.

God will not bless you with more if you are not faithful with the little you already have. Expect God to bless you in the best way possible. The Bible tells us that He will do exceedingly above what we ask:

> Now to Him who is able to do far more abundantly beyond all that we ask or think, according to the power that works within us, to Him be the glory in the church and in Christ Jesus to all generations forever and ever. Amen.
>
> —EPHESIANS 3:20–21

When we trust God with our finances and yield them to Him, then God can cause our finances to grow. Trust Him with the little you have and watch Him multiply it. Many people are in poor financial shape because they lack wisdom in seed sowing. The Word of God tells us to give and it shall be given to us; give little and you will reap little, give much and you will reap much.

> Now this I say, he who sows sparingly will also reap sparingly, and he who sows bountifully will also reap bountifully. Each one must do just as he has purposed in his heart, not grudgingly or under compulsion, for God loves a cheerful giver.
>
> —2 CORINTHIANS 9:6–7

> Give, and it will be given to you. They will pour into your lap a good measure—pressed down, shaken together and running over. For by your standard of measure it will be measured to you in return.
>
> —LUKE 6:38

You will reap more than what you sowed. Each person's measure of giving is different. One person may give ten cents and that is a lot to him because that may be all he has. On the other hand, another person may give one thousand dollars out of his abundance. The one who gave ten cents gave more because of his sacrifice in giving.

> And He sat down opposite the treasury, and began observing how the people were putting money into the treasury; and many rich people were putting in large sums. A poor widow came and put in two small copper coins, which amount to a cent. Calling His disciples to Him, He said to them, "Truly I say to you, this poor widow put in more than all the contributors to the treasury; for they all put in out of their surplus, but she, out of her poverty, put in all she owned, all she had to live on."
>
> —MARK 12:41–44

The one who gave ten cents trusted God with his last. He did not try to hold on to it, he planted it in the things of God. Plant your seed where it matters most, where you know you are guaranteed a good return on your investment.

God is not only concerned with your money, but your time as well. Plant your time in the things of God and He will reward you.

> Therefore be careful how you walk, not as unwise men but as wise, making the most of your time, because the days are evil. So then do not be foolish, but understand what the will of the Lord is.
>
> —EPHESIANS 5:15–17

Do not take your time for granted because it is not guaranteed that you will live a long life. We do not know when Jesus will return or when He will call us home. Make sure you are ready because the Bible says to be absent from the body is to be present before the Lord:

We are of good courage, I say, and prefer rather to be absent
from the body and to be at home with the Lord.

—2 CORINTHIANS 5:8

Chapter 14

KEY FOURTEEN: TIME IS NEAR–JESUS IS THE KEY

The time is here to prepare for the return of Christ our Lord. Get your house in order; prepare yourself for a place in heaven. Make reservations for yourself in eternity with the Father. The Bible tells us that you must be born again to see the kingdom of God: "Jesus answered and said to him, 'Truly, truly, I say to you, unless one is born again he cannot see the kingdom of God'" (John 3:3). Do not wait until the party date, the "Royal Party" when our Lord will call us into the sky to meet Him in glory.

> Then we who are alive and remain will be caught up together with them in the clouds to meet the Lord in the air, and so we shall always be with the Lord.
> —1 THESSALONIANS 4:17

> Then they will see THE SON OF MAN COMING IN CLOUDS with great power and glory. And then He will send forth the angels, and will gather together His elect from the four winds, from the farthest end of the earth to the farthest end of heaven.
> —MARK 13:26–27

The hour is near, the time is now; ask Jesus into your heart, make Him the controller of your life.

> And he said to me, "Do not seal up the words of the prophecy of this book, for *the time is near*. Let the one who

does wrong, still do wrong; and the one who is filthy, still
be filthy; and let the one who is righteous, still practice
righteousness; and the one who is holy, still keep himself
holy. Behold, I am coming quickly, and My reward is with
Me, to render to every man according to what he has done.
I am the Alpha and the Omega, the first and the last, the
beginning and the end. Blessed are those who wash their
robes, so that they may have the right to the tree of life, and
may enter by the gates into the city."
—REVELATION 22:10–14, EMPHASIS ADDED

Allow Jesus to lead you to eternal life with Him in heaven.
Streets of pearls and diamonds, where there is no death, an eternity of peace, happiness, and joy. There is no pain and suffering
for the enemy was cast out. Until then put on the armor of the
Lord, as Ephesians 6:11, 14–17 tells us to do:

Put on the full armor of God, so that you will be able
to stand firm against the schemes of the devil....Stand
firm therefore, HAVING GIRDED YOUR LOINS WITH
TRUTH, and HAVING PUT ON THE BREASTPLATE OF
RIGHTEOUSNESS, and having shod YOUR FEET WITH
THE PREPARATION OF THE GOSPEL OF PEACE; in
addition to all, taking up the shield of faith with which you
will be able to extinguish all the flaming arrows of the evil
one. And take THE HELMET OF SALVATION, and the
sword of the Spirit, which is the word of God.

Put on the whole armor of the Lord daily because He is always
with you. *Jesus is the Key to eternal life.* Amen.

Then I will set the *key of the house of David* on his shoulder,
When he opens no one will shut, When he shuts no one
will open.
—ISAIAH 22:22, EMPHASIS ADDED

And to the angel of the church in Philadelphia write: *He who is holy, who is true, who has the key of David,* who opens and no one will shut, and who shuts and no one opens, says this: "I know your deeds. Behold, I have put before you an open door which no one can shut, because you have a little power, and have kept My word, and have not denied My name. Behold, I will cause those of the synagogue of Satan, who say that they are Jews and are not, but lie—I will make them come and bow down at your feet, and make them know that I have loved you. Because you have kept the word of My perseverance, I also will keep you from the hour of testing, that hour which is about to come upon the whole world, to test those who dwell on the earth. I am coming quickly; hold fast what you have, so that no one will take your crown. He who overcomes, I will make him a pillar in the temple of My God, and he will not go out from it anymore; and I will write on him the name of My God, and the name of the city of My God, the new Jerusalem, which comes down out of heaven from My God, and My new name.

—REVELATION 3:7–12, EMPHASIS ADDED

Just as it was in the days of Noah, so also will it be in the days of the Son of Man. People were eating, drinking, marrying and being given in marriage up to the day Noah entered the ark. Then the flood came and destroyed them all. It was the same in the days of Lot. People were eating and drinking, buying and selling, planting and building. But the day Lot left Sodom, fire and sulfur rained down from heaven and destroyed them all. It will be just like this on the day the Son of Man is revealed. On that day no one who is on the housetop, with possessions inside, should go down to get them. Likewise, no one in the field should go back for anything. Remember Lot's wife. Whoever tries to keep their life will lose it, and whoever loses their life will preserve it. I tell you, on that night two people will be in one bed; one will be taken and the other left. Two women will be grinding grain together; one will be taken and the other left.

—LUKE 17:26–36, NIV

JESUS IS THE KEY

The heavens declare the glory of God; the skies proclaim the work of his hands.

Day after day they pour forth speech; night after night they display knowledge.

There is no speech or language where their voice is not heard.

Their voice goes out into all the earth, their words to the ends of the world.

In the heavens he has pitched a tent for the sun, which is like a bridegroom coming forth from his pavilion, like a champion rejoicing to run his course.

It rises at one end of the heavens and makes its circuit to the other; nothing is hidden from its heat.

The law of the LORD is perfect, reviving the soul.

The statutes of the LORD are trustworthy, making wise the simple.

The precepts of the LORD are right, giving joy to the heart.

The commands of the LORD are radiant, giving light to the eyes.

The fear of the LORD is pure, enduring forever.

The ordinances of the LORD are sure and altogether righteous.

They are more precious than gold, than much pure gold; they are sweeter than honey, than honey from the comb.

By them is your servant warned; in keeping them there is great reward.

Who can discern his errors? Forgive my hidden faults.

Keep your servant also from willful sins; may they not rule over me.

Then will I be blameless, innocent of great transgression.

May the words of my mouth and the meditation of my heart be pleasing in your sight,

O LORD, my Rock and my Redeemer.

—PSALM 19, NIV

TESTIMONY OF GOD'S GOODNESS AND FAITHFULNESS

This is my testimony of how this book, *The Key to Eternity*, came into existence. On December 22, 1999, I had a night vision of a book. The title of the book was *The Key to Eternity*. I knew the vision was from God, so I awoke and asked God if this was a book that He wanted me to write. That same night, I had a dream of a coworker telling me who would do the illustrations for the book design that I was to write. This second revelation was an answer to my prayer. I asked God if He was telling me to write this book to make it plain to me. I wanted to be obedient to Him. I was willing to write the book, but only if He (God) would be the author because I was a nurse and not a writer. I would obey God if He would tell me what to write about. I had no idea what God wanted me to write about. I trusted Him and I would do what He said.

Shortly after the vision and dream, I committed myself to accomplish what I was instructed to do. On my off-work days, when my children went off to school, I would go upstairs into the guest bedroom. I would begin by praying to God, asking Him to lead me in writing this book. I asked for the Holy Spirit to help me. Little did I know, the Holy Spirit began to guide me on what I was to write about. I would ask the Holy Spirit what each chapter title was, then the words would flow like I was taking dictation.

As I wrote, I began to notice that much of the writings were scriptural, so I went back and plugged in the scriptures to each particular topic. I realized that I was a vessel being used by God to reach His people. He was my guide. I agreed to write if God would be the author, and He did just that.

When I began to write, I knew this would be a book to help others, and it is; but, little did I know that God would allow me to experience some things in my life that would bring Him glory and show that we can do all things through Christ who strengthens us. God helps us to live the abundant life now, while waiting for eternity with Christ. God had me write about His promises. Then ten years later, He had me write about my experiences and trials that I could tell you about that would be a testimony of the truth of God's promises.

This book is a testimony that His Word is true and alive when we believe. I cannot express to you in words how true Mark 11:23–24 is: "For assuredly, I say to you, whoever says to this mountain, 'Be removed and be cast into the sea,' and does not doubt in his heart, but believes that those things he says will be done, he will have whatever he says. Therefore, I say to you, whatever things you ask when you pray, believe that you receive them, and you will have them" (NKJV). God has proven this over and over in my life. In Mark 9:23, "Jesus said to him, 'If you can believe, all things are possible to him who believes'" (NKJV).

In November 2009, while I was asleep, the Spirit of the Lord told me that I was about to see the book published. So, I began to prepare it to be published. In December of that same year, the Spirit of the Lord told me that the book would be completed at the end of the month, and it was. After the book was completed, I prayed and asked God what publishing company I was to send the book to. I remembered in 2004 the Spirit of the Lord told me, God had anointed a publisher for the book. The Lord answered my prayer and told me again while asleep to send the manuscript to Charisma. I looked them up online and what the

Lord said happened. All the praises and glory belong to our Lord and Savior, Jesus Christ!

Many times, I had visions of the book in stores. This was God's way of encouraging me that it would be published. All things are possible with God when we believe. Everything I have written about in this book, I have experienced over the years. I am living proof that God's Word (promises) is alive and true. He does what His Word says. He watches over His Word to perform it. He has healed me several times. He has delivered me from fear and is still changing me every day.

I pray that this book will be a blessing to you, to believe on every word of God. He is faithful and true. What He has done for me, He can also do for you. He loves you and wants the very best for you. Believe that!

ABOUT THE AUTHOR

JoAnn Young is a mother of two young adults. She is married to Jerry Young. They both are ministers for the Lord and are founders of House of Prayer Ministries (www.house-of-prayer. org). They are long-time members of Lakewood Church under the leadership of Pastors Joel and Victoria Osteen, where JoAnn has served in volunteer ministry. JoAnn and Jerry are both registered nurses. JoAnn has a bachelor's degree in Ministry Leadership from the College of Biblical Studies, Houston, Texas. They recently moved to Eunice, Louisiana, to continue ministering God's Word and to plant a Christian church.

CONTACT THE AUTHOR

HOUSE OF PRAYER MINISTRIES
P.O. BOX 1383
EUNICE, LA 70535
337–466–3320

IF YOU WOULD LIKE TO SCHEDULE JOANN YOUNG AS
A SPEAKER, PLEASE CONTACT HER AT THE FOLLOWING
E-MAIL ADDRESS: JYOUNG2032@YAHOO.COM